D0252702

COME
HELP
CHANGE
THE
WORLD

COME
HELP
CHANGE
THE
WORLD

BILL BRIGHT

Fleming H. Revell Company
Old Tappan, New Jersey

Scripture quotations in this book are from the *King James Version of the Bible* unless otherwise identified. Other references used are *The Amplified New Testament*, © by The Lockman Foundation; the *New American Standard Version of the Revised Bible*—New Testament; and *Living Letters, the Paraphrased Epistles* published by Tyndale House Publishers.

SBN 8007-0388-X
Copyright © 1970 by Bill Bright
Published by Fleming H. Revell Company
All Rights Reserved
Library of Congress Catalog Card Number: 70-112462
Printed in the United States of America

To those individuals who are and have been a part of the Campus Crusade for Christ staff family, I gratefully and affectionately dedicate this book. They are twentieth century Christian disciples who are committed to changing the world and fulfilling the Great Commission in this generation. This is their story.

Contents

	Preface	9
	Foreword	11
1	Changed Men	17
2	Arrowhead—A Fabulous Dream	20
3	In the Beginning	24
4	Growing Up	30
5	Moving Out	42
6	Story of a Miracle	51
7	The Trial of Faith	61
8	The Secret: Proper Training	72
9	The Key: The Campus	79
10	A Strategy for Colleges	91
11	Berkeley—A New Kind of Revolution	97
12	Reaching High-School Students	103
13	The Lay Ministry	110
14	The Military Ministry	127
15	Athletes in Action	131
16	Multiplying the Message	140
17	All Things to All Men	149

18 Into All the World   161
19 Arrowhead Springs: A Center for Year-Round
      Action   174
20 The Importance of Follow-Up   181
21 How It Is All Financed   188
22 Come Help Change the World   194
    Organization Chart   203
    References   205

Preface

To acknowledge all the gifts of time, talent and resources which so many have given to Campus Crusade for Christ International over the past nineteen years is an impossibility. No book I have ever seen would be large enough to itemize these priceless contributions. For this reason, when Wilbur Davies of Fleming H. Revell Company asked me to write the story of Campus Crusade for Christ International some years ago, I was at first reluctant to undertake the task. In fact, while working on it during the last two years there have been occasions when I have seriously questioned the wisdom of completing it. Again and again I argued with myself. "I cannot do justice to this great demonstration of God's miraculous work," I have told different ones. However, as I pondered the phrase, "God's miraculous work," I knew that this was the key to the Crusade story, *Come Help Change the World*.

I have prayed through the years that the ministry of Campus Crusade for Christ would be characterized by the supernatural—the miraculous—so that no one would give credit to me or to the staff, but that all the glory would go to God our Savior for the great things He has done and is doing. Thus, the story of Campus Crusade could be told and had to be told, because it is not a record of man's deeds but of God's. The credit is His, not ours, and each member of the Campus Crusade for Christ staff believes this. On that basis, I have told the story to the best of my ability without fear of offending anyone because of failure to give proper credit.

In selecting material to be included, I have had only one thought in mind: its effectiveness in illustrating the work which God can do through men who have relinquished their lives to Him and who can with abandonment say, "Thy will be done, Lord. We trust You with every detail of our lives."

Therefore, I have refrained from thanking any one of the thousands of people who have been used of God to make this miraculous ministry possible. Instead, I am confident that they join me in giving all thanks, praise, adoration, worship and glory to the One who is the source of all that we have and are, the Lord Jesus Christ, Creator of heaven and earth, and man's only Savior.

BILL BRIGHT

Foreword

I first met Bill Bright in 1957 at a conference of college students. During the conference, he asked me if I would serve as a member of the advisory board for the young organization he headed, Campus Crusade for Christ. My reply was, "I don't know that much about Campus Crusade. I have always felt that a person should not lend his name to an organization unless it is reasonable and probable that he will be able to participate actively in its work."

Bill Bright had good answers. He said he wasn't in the business of collecting names, but rather was looking for persons whose backgrounds and interests indicated they would be able to help him shape the future of a vision God had given him to help bring Christ and His gospel to the world in our time and in obedience to our Lord's command. As I came to know Bright himself and looked into the activities and accomplishments of the movement, it was clear that God was at work in Campus Crusade. He was using it in this student generation as He had used the Student Volunteer Movement in mine. That organization had meant more to me personally than any other in my student days as it had sought to challenge every student to give his life to Jesus Christ and to consider Christian service in the needy parts of the world overseas. I wanted to do my utmost to support any group that would help young people today as the SVM helped me and thousands of others yesterday.

My enthusiasm for the work of Bill Bright and the ministry of Campus Crusade for Christ has grown steadily over the years.

I have observed firsthand the work and witness of Campus Crusade, how God has blessed it and expanded it. I have marveled at the quiet, steady, contagious dedication of Bill and Vonette Bright and of the people who have joined them to become a part of the army taking the gospel around the world in this generation. They, and all on their team, are warmly and winsomely evangelistic—as was Christ Himself—but are never divisive. They dream great dreams, but are completely levelheaded and practical in bringing them to fruition. And, true to his word, Bill has sought help and counsel from his advisory board members; though, more important, his ear has always been especially attuned to his No. 1 Director, the Lord Jesus Christ.

In Bill Bright's determination to help fulfill the Great Commission, I have felt on occasion that he might be expanding the scope of Campus Crusade's activities too rapidly. That was especially true when he told us of his plans to begin a vast lay ministry. I felt that it would be better to keep the original concentration on students, that this was Campus Crusade's special field, and that it might lose effectiveness if spread too wide and too thin! But once again Bill had thought the program through and the subsequent success of this broadened witness has attested to its rightness. His vision has always run ahead of most of us.

This book is a must reading for every Christian who really means business for God, for the exciting story of Campus Crusade for Christ—truly a miracle—tells what God can and will do today. It would be a tremendous story at any time because of the multitude of lives being changed for good, and there has never been anything more relevant in our age. Changing the hearts and lives of men is always "where the action" begins for changing society. But in times such as these—when disbelief seems to be routing the faith of many, when self-indulgence and pleasure and materialism seem to some to make folly of love and self-denial and commitment—Campus Crusade holds aloft a guiding beacon for the world.

For ten years I had the privilege of serving as a medical missionary for Christ in China. When our work there was closed by the Japanese invasion and Communist pressures, I served for twenty years in the United States House of Representatives as a congressman from Minnesota. Since 1962, I have sought by speaking, writing and broadcasting to alert Americans to the forces, both national and international, that seriously threaten not only our, but the world's future peace and well-being—issues especially relevant to our times—and how best to deal with them.

Naturally, I have had contact with many kinds of people and organizations, both secular and religious. I have never met anyone more committed to any cause than is Bill Bright to the fulfilling of the Great Commission in our generation, and he has concrete, responsible plans to support his convictions. Nor do I know of any other such phenomenal movement for Christ in our time as Campus Crusade. Its past performance gives convincing evidence that it will—by God's grace and continued dependence upon the Holy Spirit—fulfill its objectives.

A few years ago the *Los Angeles Times* said of this ministry, "No movement of our time is likely to have a healthier effect on the religious life in America." The story told in this book supports eloquently the truth of that statement. Any person who may be troubled by the assertions in some circles that God is dead or never was, will find in this story that God is very much alive indeed, and at work, and that "His touch has still its ancient power."

We need to learn of and wholeheartedly ally ourselves with this vital Crusade.

WALTER H. JUDD

COME
HELP
CHANGE
THE
WORLD

1

Changed Men

As the president of a large, international movement I am involved with thousands of others in a "conspiracy to overthrow the world." Each year we train tens of thousands of high school and college students from more than half of the major countries of the world in the art of revolution, and daily these "revolutionists" are at work around the globe, spreading our philosophy and strengthening and broadening our influence.

Today, below my office window hundreds of students are milling about outside our administration building, sharing a passion that has gripped them all. For example, I see George over near a tree. Just a few months ago, George was a member of Students for a Democratic Society (SDS). He hated everything about America and was determined to help destroy the "establishment." He had committed his life to raping the status quo. In his mind he carried a list of public officials who were his to eliminate—to kill when the revolution came. So far as he was concerned, the time for such action was now. Then one day he came into contact with some of the New Folk, a singing group in our organization. They sang of a revolution, too, but it was entirely different in its approach, and George came over to our side.

Then there is Julie in that group of girls over there. She's the beauty with dark hair. A year ago she was an acid head, completely hung up on LSD, and did anything to get money enough to maintain her habit. What she did was sell herself to any man who had the price. Several times she considered suicide, and one time she tried and almost succeeded. Then, a member of our staff met her and told her about a way out of her bondage. She, too, became a part of our movement.

I don't see a boy named Joe out front, but he's there, somewhere. He comes from one of the nation's first families. His forebears were pioneers who arrived here shortly after the Pilgrims. Unfortunately, his parents were divorced when he was quite young and he was raised by a grandmother who was unable to "communicate" with her grandson. Because of his loneliness and in spite of the great wealth and prestige of the family name, he decided to chuck it all and become a hippie. As such he thought—for a while—that he had found meaning to life. He cut off all contact with his family for nearly two years, living a sordid life which eventually became revolting even to him. One of our staff met him and talked with him just after he was coming off a horrible overdose drug trip. When he heard that there was another way to "turn on" to life he listened and agreed to give it a try. Today, he is one of our most enthusiastic "revolutionaries."

In that group of five or six sitting on the grass over beyond that little rise, the black face belongs to a fellow named Steve. His hatred for white people knew no bounds. He was the most militant of the militants and his group involved itself in every destructive plot imaginable, biding time until the big showdown when the white man would be made to suffer the indignities his people had experienced. Then, one day Steve met the most beautiful girl he had ever seen. Added to the beauty of her features was a beauty of spirit, which shone from deep within. This girl, also on our team, opened Steve's eyes to a different kind of revolution and he, too, found a new cause.

As I study the scene before me, I think of the hundreds of university and college presidents across the nation who have looked down upon other student gatherings during the past few years. Often they have been filled with fear and anxiety as young men and women vented their frustrations with either threats of violence or overt violence itself. The press has well documented—maybe too well—the riots, the plunderings, the burnings, the bloodshed and even the murders that have left many of the nation's campuses in shambles.

Fortunately, the students before me are in a different mood—

now. It is true that some of the "revolutionaries" before me have been recruited from among the ringleaders of these uprisings. I know many of them and their backgrounds. But most of these young people are not campus rowdies, but rather are sharp, intelligent young people. Many of them are student body presidents, class officers, honor students, outstanding athletes and other student leaders.

What is this cause that grips these young people? What is their revolution? It is a revolution of love and reason, and their leader is Jesus Christ. The revolution in which they are engaged is under the auspices of Campus Crusade for Christ International. Campus Crusade is a worldwide movement totally dedicated to one goal: to help fulfill the Great Commission of our Lord by taking the claims of Christ to the millions of students in every country of the world, and, through them and a trained adult leadership, to help saturate each country of the world with the good news of God's love and forgiveness in Christ. Our special emphasis (though it is not our total thrust) is on the college and high school campuses, because we believe that it is here that the main source of untapped manpower waits to be challenged and trained to help change the world.

2

Arrowhead— A Fabulous Dream

"This is a fabulous place and it would be an ideal headquarters for us," I told my good friend George Rowan, "but I am sure that it is far beyond our means. What is the lowest price the owner would take?"

"He is asking two million, firm," George replied. I swallowed hard. This was an incredible amount for our organization, which had never had an extra dollar in its ten years of existence. Now, even though we had expanded to the point that we had to have more and larger facilities, I could not truthfully conceive of any way that we could raise the kind of money that would be needed to make such a large purchase.

I had come to Arrowhead Springs, in the foothills above San Bernardino, California, assuming that this former hotel would have deteriorated considerably from the plush days when it was hosting some of the biggest names in the entertainment and business world. To my surprise it was all in amazingly good condition. Except for a little peeling paint on the outside of the six-story building, there seemed to be little wrong with it. One could not really haggle too much over a little paint! The two million dollar figure was a good one—only a fraction of the property's true worth. It had been appraised at $6,700,000. The beds were even made; spare linens were in the closets; china, silverware and cooking utensils (about $450,000 in inventory) were ready and waiting for guests. "All we would have to do would be to move in," I thought. The resort didn't look as though it had been closed most of the time for almost four years, but it had.

I knew that the hotel had been closed, and had heard about its availability but hadn't bothered to investigate. I knew it was out of our reach financially. In fact, from the time our work had begun we had had only enough money for our daily needs, so that any amount would have been too much. But when someone suggested that the owners were anxious to sell at such a low price, I decided to send Gordon Klenck, who had been on our staff since its second year and was then my personal assistant (he is now our European director), to investigate the property and see if he thought we could convert it into a Campus Crusade training headquarters. Gordon, who is very conservative and not given to exaggeration, came back from a visit to Arrowhead Springs, his eyes aglow. Without batting an eye he said, "This facility would revolutionize our ministry and increase our outreach a hundredfold."

"Okay, Gordon, I will have a look myself," I responded, and arrangements were made for my visit to Arrowhead Springs with George Rowan, a Los Angeles businessman. Meanwhile, I did a little research and learned several interesting things about the famous resort.

For example, I learned that various Indian tribes had come to this spot through the centuries, bringing their sick and wounded for healing in the natural hot mineral springs. They called the place "holy land," and all weapons of warfare were laid aside here. The first hotel and spa was built on the property in 1854 by Dr. David Noble Smith and was widely advertised as a health resort. When the original hotel was destroyed by fire, two others followed. They were razed and the present structure of concrete and steel was built in 1939, financed by a group of Hollywood film stars. It opened in December of that year. Present for the gala opening were some of the biggest names in Hollywood and the business world. Rudy Vallee, Al Jolson and Judy Garland entertained on that first night.

Arrowhead Springs became a popular retreat for the movie colony and for top executives in the business world. Only a short distance from the heart of Los Angeles (today only sixty minutes by freeway), world-famous movie stars streamed toward Arrowhead Springs for relaxation and revelry. Esther Williams' swimming classics were filmed in the extravagantly designed cabana pool, which cost $125,000 to build before World War II, and would cost over $500,000 today.

However, when transportation developed to the point that the stars could easily travel further afield, they were attracted to Las Vegas and Palm Springs; Arrowhead Springs turned into something of a white elephant. Several different owners tried to restore the property to the status it had once enjoyed, but without any noticeable success. Finally, Benjamin Swig, owner of the Fairmount Hotel in San Francisco and the historic Mission Inn in Riverside, California, acquired it from the Hilton Foundation. He operated it briefly, before concluding, as had his predecessors, that it had limited profit potential, and he closed it down. Though different groups tried to purchase it from Mr. Swig, and one or two parties used it for a brief time, it was closed more than it was open during the approximately four years before my visit.

When I first arrived in 1961, I was immediately enchanted by the remoteness of the property. Following a winding road into the hills above San Bernardino, I was reeling with the grandeur of Arrowhead Springs before I ever stepped out of Mr. Rowan's automobile. I was even more impressed as I walked about the spacious grounds and examined the many buildings.

Below me, a couple of miles away, spread the populated valley, feverishly at work—industry clanging and pounding, cars and trucks rumbling in every direction. But all I could hear was the song of birds, the rustle of date palm leaves as the wind filtered gently through them, and the sound of rushing water from a stream as it made its way from many artesian springs, tumbling wildly down over the rocks into Strawberry Canyon.

But even these sounds were muted. In a way, an ethereal quality permeated the place and more than once I found myself almost whispering to Mr. Rowan as we walked the grounds, 1,735 acres in all. There were ten private bungalows, dormitory facilities for several hundred, an auditorium which could accommodate 700 people, a recreation house, four tennis courts, a stable, two big swimming pools and the 136-room six-story hotel. Without too much imagination, I could see as many as a thousand people here at one time. At Mound, Minnesota, where we had been conducting most of our summer institutes for evangelism, approximately 150

22

people were all we could crowd in at one time, even with wall-to-wall-people.

Could this be the answer to our dilemma—our need for larger training facilities? I wondered. Constrained to be alone, to talk with the Lord, I asked Mr. Rowan to excuse me while I went into the hotel alone.

Past the unattended reception desk, through the empty lobby, out into the glass-enclosed Wanhi Room I moved, the click of my shoes echoing as I walked. There was a shiny bar, empty of customers. Behind it the glasses were stacked, awaiting business. The shelves, where a goodly supply of bottles once stood, were now empty. Tables and chairs were grouped in intimate clusters so that holidayers could look out on the city, which I could imagine would be a starry wonder at night. But it was broad daylight at that moment, and I had not come there for a drink or to see the panoramic view, but to share with the Lord the dream that was working overtime in my head.

Falling to my knees, I bowed my head and began praying—and listening. "I am overwhelmed, Lord. This place is so big and beautiful. True, we've been asking You to direct us to new facilities, the best place in the country, and I know that You will; but, if this is it, where will we get $2,000,000 to buy it? It seems too impossible to even consider. Yet I keep hearing in my heart Your voice and it suggests that this is the place You want us to have. If it is, then You are going to have to make it crystal clear. How can I know for sure?"

Then, though not in an audible voice, God spoke to me as clearly as if there had been a public address system in the room. Unmistakably, I heard Him say, "I have been saving this for Campus Crusade for Christ. I want you to have it, and I will supply the funds to pay for it."

With tears running down my face, I said, "God, I don't know how You intend to work this miracle, but I know You can, and I thank You for this gift. I claim this property in Your name."

3

In the Beginning

How and when we would acquire the fabulous Arrowhead Springs property were mysteries to me; yet, I was inwardly assured that it would happen, and I left the grounds that day in 1961 with the joyful anticipation of that coming day. But I am getting ahead of myself. Perhaps I should take you back to the beginning of the Campus Crusade for Christ story, to that moment when God revealed to me in dramatic fashion the ministry I was to undertake for Him.

It was the spring of the year 1951, my senior year at Fuller Theological Seminary. For two exciting and happy years I had been married to my hometown sweetheart, the former Vonette Zachary. Vonette had accepted a teaching position in the Los Angeles school system, and we found ourselves living a very busy and eventful life. Once or twice a week, in addition to regular meetings at church, I had the privilege of leading a deputation group of more than a hundred dedicated college and post-college age young men and women who wanted to become disciples for the Lord Jesus Christ. We covered approximately thirty assignments each month, visiting the local jails and hospitals, skid row missions, and wherever we felt we were needed. I soon discovered that we had to wait our turn to go to jail services and skid row missions because there were many other churches covering this area of service. One day it occurred to me that there were no waiting lines to reach college students or the top executives of the city. Here were the neglected leaders of our world, both today's and tomorrow's!

By this time Vonette and I had become increasingly aware that living for Christ and serving Him was our major goal in life. As a result of this awareness, one Sunday afternoon we decided we would sign a contract with the Lord. No one had ever suggested this; it was just something we decided to do together. Both of us had been very ambitious and very materialistic and had lived typically selfish lives prior to becoming Christians. Now the Lord had changed us and had given us a love for Himself and a desire to serve Him and others.

So, Vonette went into one room, and I into another, in our home in the Hollywood hills, and we made a list of all the things we had wanted out of life. When I had first proposed to Vonette, we had once talked about a honeymoon in Europe, about securing the finest voice teacher to develop her already beautiful singing voice, and about living in the fabulous Bel-Air district of Los Angeles. But now all that had been given to Christ. Such ambitions had become secondary, if not nonexistent (not that they are wrong goals in themselves, but for us there was no longer a great appetite for them). So, we made a new list of the things we wanted.

Our new lists, surprisingly alike, included: (1) to live holy lives, controlled and empowered by the Holy Spirit; (2) to be fruitful in our witness for Christ; and (3) to help to fulfill the Great Commission in our generation. We were also concerned for a Christian home, and we suggested two to four children (we have two boys). We thought it would be convenient to own two cars. Today we don't own any, but God has provided us transportation through the generosity of a friend who is also interested in reaching the world for Christ. And, we mentioned in our list, if the Lord be pleased, a home nice enough for entertaining the President of the United States and modest enough that a man from Skid Row would feel comfortable in it.

By now we had begun to respond to the command of our Lord: "But seek ye first the kingdom of God, and his righteousness . . ." [1] We believed that God's will was better than our own. The more we knew of God's love for us, of his wisdom, power and grace, the more we could trust Him. So we signed our names to these lists as a formal act of commitment to Christ and His cause. This was

[1] References appear at back of book.

25

a particularly significant commitment inasmuch as we were doing it together as a young husband and wife. There was no particular emotion involved. It was simply a transaction of the will. Of course, we had been motivated to do this on the basis of the Spirit of God working in us, as explained through the Apostle Paul, "For it is God which worketh in you both to will and to do of his good pleasure." [2]

What was to happen as a result of this commitment we did not know, but I am sure that God did; and, within a few short months, as we continued studies, teaching, deputation work, and business, His plans began to unfold.

About the midnight hour, one night in the final semester of my senior year in the seminary, I was studying for a Greek exam with Hugh Brom, a classmate. We were seated at a desk in our living room. There was nothing unusual about the setting or about the circumstances. Vonette was asleep in a nearby room. Suddenly, without warning or without any indication of what was going to happen, I sensed the presence of God in a way I had never known before. It was even more real than the later Arrowhead Springs revelation. Though it could not have lasted more than a few seconds, I suddenly had the overwhelming impression that the Lord had unfolded a scroll of instructions of what I was to do with my life.

It is difficult to talk about such experiences for fear of being misunderstood or causing others to seek after such an experience; but I think I know a little something of what the Apostle Paul experienced on his way to Damascus.[3] In any event, this was the greatest spiritual experience of my Christian life. At this time and in a very definite way, God commanded me to invest my life in helping to fulfill the Great Commission in this generation, specifically through winning and discipling the students of the world for Christ. How to do this was not spelled out in detail; that came later as the Lord gave additional insights for the implementation of the original vision. When I tried to tell Hugh what had happened, he did not understand, though he was very sympathetic and rejoiced with me. I was reminded of those who were with the Apostle Paul when he met Christ on the Damascus road. They did not understand all that was happening either. After Hugh had gone, I awakened Vonette and together we praised God for His direction and promised that with His grace and strength we would obey Him.

Though my heart was filled with praise and thanksgiving to the Lord for this remarkable revelation of what I was to do with my life, I still needed the counsel of more mature Christians. The next day I went to see one of my favorite seminary professors, Dr. Wilbur Smith, famous scholar and author of many books. As I shared with him what God had revealed to me, he got out of his chair and paced back and forth in his office, saying again and again, "This is of God. This is of God. I want to help you. Let me think and pray about it."

The next morning when I arrived for his seven o'clock class in English Bible, Dr. Smith called me out of the classroom into a little counseling room and handed me a piece of paper on which he had scribbled these letters, "CCC." He explained that God had indeed provided the name for my vision.

Ever since that spring night experience, it has been my passion and concern to be obedient to the heavenly vision that God had given me, even going so far as to drop out of seminary with only a few units remaining before graduation. I became convinced, and remain so convinced today, that God did not want me to be ordained. Though I have a great respect and appreciation for clergy, layman status has often worked to a great advantage in my ministry with students and laymen.

The next move was to look for a board of outstanding men and women of God to advise and counsel me in the establishment of this ministry. Dr. Wilbur Smith was the first I approached. Then I asked Dr. Henrietta Mears (who had helped to introduce both Vonette and me to Christ), Billy Graham, Dick Halverson, Dawson Trotman, Cy Nelson, Dan Fuller, and Edwin Orr, to serve in this capacity. All of them readily agreed to be a part of this new facet of God's strategy. The events of the days that followed were framed in prayer and meditation. The guidance I was seeking was *where to begin.* "Lord, where do You want us to launch this ministry?" was a prayer Vonette and I and our friends uttered frequently in the spring and summer of 1951.

Increasingly, the University of California at Los Angeles was the focus of our attention. It seemed so right to begin there, at a university that in 1951 had a strong, radical minority which was exercising great influence and was causing unprecedented disturbances. Many referred to the campus as "the little Red school house." It seemed that this would be one of the most difficult campuses on which to begin, and that if our venture for Christ could succeed there, it would be likely to succeed on any campus.

One of our first steps was to look for a place to live near the UCLA campus. Rents were extremely high, and nothing was readily available in the immediate vicinity. But we kept searching and praying that God would lead us to the right location.

One day as I was going over the files with a local realtor, he turned past the listing of a large home only one block from the campus with a rental of $450 per month, which in 1951 was astronomical. Our budget indicated that we would be able to spend up to $200, though that was more than we could realistically afford to pay. Yet when the realtor flipped the card to the listing of this house, I told him rather emphatically, "That's the house. I want to see it."

"Why?" he asked. "They are asking more than twice the amount you are willing to pay."

But I continued to press him. "How long has the house been listed?"

"For several months." Then he explained how two maiden sisters lived in the house and were planning to take a South American tour. "As a matter of fact," he observed, studying the card, "they leave next week."

I asked permission to go to see them, and I found the house ideally suited for our needs. It was located approximately one block from the sorority row and had plenty of room, in particular a spacious living room where I could visualize us holding large group sessions. I explained to the owners our interest in reaching the students of UCLA for Christ, and that we would not be able to pay more than $200 a month. They said that they would think about it and would call us. By the time I returned to our home in Hollywood, they had called. Impressed with our mission and wanting to have a part in it, they agreed to the $200 a month rent if we would pay an additional $25 a month for the gardener. This we agreed to do, and shortly thereafter we moved into our new home in Westwood.

Our first spiritual effort was to organize a twenty-four-hour chain of prayer divided into ninety-six periods of fifteen minutes each and invite people to pray around the clock that God would do a unique thing on the UCLA campus. Next, we began to recruit and train interested students and to organize them into teams to visit the various fraternities and sororities, dormitories, and other groups on the campus. The teams would present personal testimonies of faith in Christ, explaining who Christ is, why He came and how others could know Him personally.

I remember well our first sorority meeting. It was at the Kappa Alpha Theta sorority, which was known then as the "house of beautiful women." Apparently the pledges were selected, among other reasons, for their good looks and personalities. In any event, when I finished my message and the challenge was presented to receive Christ, many girls remained behind to talk to us and ask further questions. It was a new experience for me. For more than a year we had gone into various fraternity and sorority houses on local campuses prior to the time that God gave the vision of this ministry; yet we had never seen one single person commit his life to Christ. To our knowledge, no one had ever prayed to receive Christ as a result of any of our meetings.

At the conclusion of this first sorority meeting following the vision God had given, I was amazed to see such a large group of young women standing in line to express their desire to become Christians. One after another they came (more than half of the original sixty girls present) communicating in different words, "I want to become a Christian." It was a humbling experience, seeing God work in this marvelous way. This was a dramatic confirmation to me that the vision to reach the collegians of the world was truly from God. Unsure, stepping carefully, speaking reservedly, we had been cautious up till then; but God seemed to be urging us forward, filling us with badly needed confidence and assurance that, having called us to this ministry, he was with us.

We invited the girls to join us the next evening for a meeting in our home nearby, and several of the young women brought their boyfriends. It was a memorable and exciting night. The boys were skeptical, but they came with the girls from "the house of beautiful women," and many of them decided for Christ too.

4

Growing Up

The days that followed demonstrated again and again the fact that God's hand was upon us and upon our ministry. In meeting after meeting—in fraternities, sororities, dormitories and with student leaders—the phenomenal response appeared to be approximately the same as that at our first meeting. The men were even more responsive than the women. In the course of a few months more than 250 students at UCLA—including the student body president, the editor of the newspaper and a number of the top athletes —committed their lives to Christ. So great was their influence for Christ on the entire campus that the chimes began to play Christian hymns at noonday.

By this time the news of what God was doing at UCLA had spread to other campuses, and students, faculty, laymen, and pastors in various parts of the country were asking, "Will you help us? We would like to start Campus Crusade for Christ at our school." At this point I had to make a very important decision. The vision that God had given to me originally embraced the whole world. If I were to stay at UCLA and devote all of my own personal energies to reach only one campus, I would be disobedient to that heavenly vision. I had fallen in love with the students and could' have easily spent the rest of my life serving Christ on that one campus. Yet there was only one thing for me to do—recruit and train other people to help reach all of the collegians of the world with the good news of God's love and forgiveness in Christ.

As in any expanding business that needs new personnel, we

30

needed a special type of man. We needed dedicated, qualified men who could articulate their faith; and we needed many of them. I assumed that they would be available by the score, if not by the hundred. The standards we established were high, of necessity. The first requirement for potential staff was that they be fruitful in their witness for Christ; second, that the individual be a seminary graduate; and third, that he be sympathetic with what we were attempting to accomplish in winning, building and sending men to help evangelize the world for our Savior. Vonette and I prayed much about the urgency to expand to other campuses. Finally, it was agreed that she would remain in charge of the work at UCLA while I went from campus to campus on a recruiting tour which took me to many of the leading Christian schools and seminaries of the nation, looking for new staff people. Imagine my disappointment when I discovered that there were just not many individuals, with or without degrees, who were fruitful for Christ and available; and that there were practically none with bachelor of divinity degrees who were effective in their witness for Christ, and who wanted to be a part of our ministry. Consequently, we were forced to change the requirements for our staff. We concluded that we would accept for campus staff those with college degrees who were otherwise qualified and who had a teachable spirit, willingness to learn how to introduce others to Christ.

After considerable recruiting, however, we did find six choice people. Two of them, Dan Fuller and Calvin Herriott, had been fellow seminarians of mine, and had just recently graduated. There were also Roe Brooks, a seminarian in his middle year; Gordon Klenck, who was just graduating from college; and Roger Aiken and Wayno Arolla, both of whom had college degrees.

Gordon Klenck was the first of these staff members to arrive in Los Angeles. He still needed to complete one course, which he was doing by correspondence, before he would receive his coveted degree. I had interviewed him on campus and was impressed with his sincerity and his dedication to Christ, though he did look extremely young. He was actually twenty years old, but he didn't look a day over seventeen.

Somehow in our correspondence we had failed to give him our telephone number and our home address. He had only a post office box number for Campus Crusade for Christ; thus, when he arrived in Los Angeles he did not know how to get in touch with us. We were still such a small organization that we had not even listed Campus Crusade for Christ in the telephone directory. Our dining room was our office, and our dining room table doubled as my desk. So, Gordon checked in at the YMCA and mailed a card to us, saying that we could find him there. He told us that if he were not in the "Y" he would be in the library completing his correspondence course. Sure enough, when we tried to locate him, we could not find him at the "Y," but upon proceeding to the library we spotted him immediately in the main reading room.

Gordon returned home with us, and as soon as we had walked into the house he asked for a card table, insisting that he must finish his correspondence course before we began our staff training. He must have sensed he would never get back to his own work once we began to train him for staff. As he set his typewriter on the card table and continued his studies, I remember Vonette commenting to me, as she noted his youthful appearance, "Do you expect to change the world with people like that?" I am sure that Gordon must have looked at us and wondered at the same time if he hadn't made a serious mistake in coming to help us!

Roe Brooks was the next to join us around the family table. "Family" is the right word to use, because we were a family, not only a family in Christ, but a family in experience. We ate together and we shared together; and our love for each other was a very real experience. Vonette tried to cook for all of us and was never sure how many guests would show up at dinnertime. But somehow we managed, cutting pork chops in two, or adding a can of soup to the stew. Amazingly, no one ever seemed to go away hungry.

Among other things, since we held so many meetings in fraternities, sororities and dormitories, it was important that all of us observe proper etiquette, be well-mannered, understand proper eating procedures, and know how to conduct ourselves in the presence of the opposite sex. Therefore, Vonette and I began to conduct a little training course for the staff. Vonette was the chief drill instructor, and we had some very profitable (and often very humorous) times together.

From the very beginning of Campus Crusade for Christ, we

have strongly emphasized the importance of the ministry of the Holy Spirit—how to appropriate by faith His power for a holy life and fruitful witness. We have also considered it important that each staff member understand how to communicate his faith in Christ to the student world in the most effective way possible. So we began to explore together the ways to accomplish this two-fold objective. During that first summer, Vonette and I spent several weeks giving these young men intensive training, the pattern of which has been amplified and developed throughout the succeeding years.

In the fall of 1952, we saw the ministry established on additional campuses, including San Diego State, University of Southern California, University of California at Berkeley, Oregon State and Washington University.

Staff members were to be paid a salary of $100 a month for nine months only. During the other three months, they would receive no remuneration at all. Obviously, they had not come because of a large salary but because they wanted to be a part of something bigger than themselves; they wanted to help to change the world. For the first several years, Vonette and I received no remuneration from Campus Crusade for Christ; rather, we were giving of what we had to help accelerate and expand the ministry.

There were many opportunities to trust the Lord. One day a wire came from Brazil from the owners of the home we had leased for a year, stating that even though only six months had passed they were ready to return home. Would we be willing to relinquish the house? As I was sitting at the table reading the wire, the telephone rang. Dr. J. Edwin Orr, internationally known evangelist and author, was calling to ask if I knew of anyone who would be interested in living in his home during the next year while he would be on world-wide evangelistic tours. It just happened that I did know someone! We made Dr. Orr's house our headquarters for three semesters, and, although it was two miles from campus, it proved to be ideal for this next phase of our UCLA ministry.

We continued to hold many fraternity, sorority and dormitory meetings, confronting hundreds of students on several campuses with the claims of Christ. Scores were responding, and once again

33

we were pressed for space. Day after day, on my way to the campus, I passed a large home of Moorish castle style architecture with a "For Sale" sign on the lawn. This home happened to be located in the famous Bel-Air district of Westwood Village directly across Sunset Boulevard from the UCLA campus. I had promised Vonette when we were married that one day we would live in Bel-Air, so I was tempted again and again to stop and inquire about it. However, I rejected the idea as being a personal, selfish desire until one day I became convinced that perhaps God did want us to acquire this property, inasmuch as it was located only about three minutes from the heart of the UCLA campus. I decided to stop and investigate the property. The price was far too much for us I discovered (every penny of ours had been invested in the ministry of reaching students for Christ), and I put the idea out of my mind.

However, shortly after my conversation with the owner, our good friend Dr. Henrietta Mears learned of our interest in the property and told us that she had been interested in and had actually negotiated for the purchase of the house some years previously. Now she would like to purchase it as her home, provided we would come to live with her, carrying our share of the expenses, of course. She explained that since the recent death of her sister Margaret with whom she had lived for many years in a large, two-story home near the UCLA campus, her house was much, much too big for her alone. Dr. Mears and Vonette accompanied me as I visited the "castle" again, and we unanimously agreed that this would be ideal for all of us, for Dr. Mears, for Vonette and me, and for the ministry of Campus Crusade for Christ. The house was large and so designed that we all had our privacy, yet could be together for our meals and whenever else we wished. Once again, God had provided for our needs.

The purchase followed, and soon we were happily and comfortably established in our new home and headquarters. Within days, students were pouring into 110 Stone Canyon Road. As many as 300 students could be packed into the spacious rooms with all of the furniture pushed aside. Scores were introduced to Christ, many of them in the little prayer room off the foyer. Sharing the Bel-Air home with Dr. Mears was made all the more meaningful to us because she had played such an important role in introducing both Vonette and me to Christ.

Perhaps I should elaborate a bit more about Dr. Mears and the part she played in my life. Apart from the example of my mother's life and prayers, she, more than any other person, was responsible for my becoming a Christian, and except for her Vonette may never have taken that spiritual step through which I have had the benefit of her love, counsel and encouragement through the rich, exciting and fruitful years of this ministry.

Vonette grew up in the same town as I did in Oklahoma. She was most attractive, intelligent and personable. She came from a fine family and I was much impressed with her. She was also very active in the church and I assumed that she was a vital Christian. However, since she was four years younger than I, I had never been even slightly interested in her until I moved away and was making my way in Los Angeles. Then, through a series of rather unusual experiences, I got in touch with her, fell in love, proposed, and before I knew it we were planning the wedding date. Yet, there was one thing that bothered me: the question of her dedication to the Lord. I had decided to enter seminary and I remember, in particular, a trip that I made to Oklahoma en route to Princeton in the fall of 1946 in order to discuss this with her.

During our time together I made the statement that God would have to come first in our marriage, and this annoyed Vonette. "I'm not sure that's right. I think a man's family should be his first concern," she bristled. I began to mount an argument, but then dropped it, thinking that there would be plenty of time to iron out this difference later. In the fall of 1947 I transferred from Princeton to Fuller Theological Seminary in California in order to be closer to my business (Bright's California Confections—a fancy food line) and was proceeding toward a degree when the matter of Vonette's personal relationship with Christ began to trouble me again. I became increasingly concerned for her spiritually. Yet I was such a young Christian and thus too immature to help her because of our emotional involvement. By this time we had been engaged for more than two years. Yet, there was the gnawing question in my mind: Was it true, as I had originally been impressed to believe, that God had chosen Vonette to be my wife? If God rules in the affairs of men and nations, and not even a sparrow falls to the ground without His knowledge, and even the hairs of our heads are numbered, it seemed to me then, as it does today, that God does have one particular mate for us. Although I had dated many girls prior to our engagement, and had been infatuated with some, I had never proposed to anyone else. I had been impressed, I felt, by the Lord, and was confident even before our first date that Vonette was the one with whom I was to share my life and my ministry for Christ. Yet, since my proposal and her acceptance, we had both become aware that she was not a Christian. Since she had never received Christ as her Savior, she could not possibly share my vision and concern about introducing others to Christ.

This was one of the greatest conflicts of my life. What was I to do? I had committed my life to Christ and His service. My one great desire was to live and, if need be, die for Him. Now I was in love with and engaged to a girl who was not even a Christian. Obviously, we could not marry if she did not become a Christian, and yet, I had been so sure. This conflict continued to persist until we decided that perhaps we should explore the possibility that God might have other plans for us. So we both began to date other people. I dated girls who were vitally interested in living for Christ; Vonette, I suppose, dated fellows who were less interested in the Lord. But we kept in touch through frequent letters and telephone calls from Los Angeles to Denton, Texas, where she was in school.

Finally, the day of graduation came for Vonette, and she received her degree in home economics from Texas Women's University. I suggested that she visit her brother, who lived nearby in Southern California. She apparently thought that this was a good idea, a sort of do-or-die time when we would decide either yes or no. Vonette, as she later told me, confided in a girl friend before she left college, "I am either going to rescue him from this religious fanaticism or come back without a ring." She did neither.

While in California, Vonette went with me to a meeting of several hundred students at a College Briefing Conference at Forest Home, the famous conference center for Christian leadership established by Dr. Mears. Even though I had been able to help many others find Christ, I felt inadequate in introducing Vonette to Him. Someone else would have to help me, and Dr. Mears was the logical choice. She had counseled with thousands of young people and knew how to communicate with individuals with inquiring and scientific minds.

By this time Vonette had begun to doubt the Bible and even the existence of God, so I felt that she needed help from someone who knew more than I. Also, because of the emotional involvement I was afraid that I might be able to get from her a verbal commitment to Christ but not a commitment of the will to Him. She might say *yes* to Christ with her lips in order to please me and not mean it in her heart.

We arrived at the beautiful mountain setting where thousands of lives had been changed. Vonette could not help but be impressed with so many vibrant lives. She liked the quality of life they possessed but was bewildered by their expressions of faith. After a couple of days she decided that they were enthusiastic about Christianity just because it was new to them. After all, she had been reared in the church and did not see anything about Christianity to get excited about. She thought their enthusiasm would soon wear off. She did not want to stand in my way and suggested that since she felt that this would not work for her perhaps we should break our engagement. It was then that I asked her to talk to Dr. Mears, who had played such an important role in my own spiritual birth and growth.

Vonette later wrote her impressions of that day.

Dr. Mears was one of the most vibrant, enthusiastic personalities that I had ever met. She was waiting for me, and the entire conference staff, without my knowledge, had been praying for my conversion. Dr. Mears explained that she had taught chemistry in Minneapolis, and that she could understand how I was thinking. (I had minored in chemistry in college and everything had to be very practical and workable to me. This was one of the reasons I had questioned the validity of Christianity.) As she explained simply to me from God's Word how I could be sure that I knew God, she used terminology very familiar to me. She explained that, just as a person going into a chemistry laboratory experiment follows the table of chemical valence, so is it possible for a person to enter God's laboratory and follow His formula of knowing Him and following Him.

During the next hour she lovingly proceeded to explain to me who Christ is and how I could know Him personally. "Dr. Mears," I said, "if Jesus Christ is the way, then how do I meet Him?" Dr. Mears responded, "In Revelation 3:20, Christ says, 'Behold, I stand at the door, and knock: if any man hear my voice, and open the door, I will come in to him, and will sup with him, and he with me.' Receiving Christ is simply a matter of turning your life—your will, your emotions, your intellect—completely over to Him. John, Chapter 1, verse 12, says 'But as many as received him, to them gave he power to become the sons of God, even to them that believe on his name.' "

When Dr. Mears finished, I thought: "If what she tells me is absolutely true, I have nothing to lose and everything to gain." I bowed my head and prayed. I asked Christ to come into my heart. And at that moment, as I look back, my life began to change. God became a reality in my life. For the first time I was ready to trust Him. I became aware that my prayers were getting beyond the ceiling. I found that I had control of areas of my life that I had not been able to control before. No longer did I have to try to love people. There just seemed to be a love that flowed from within that I did not have to create. God had added a new dimension to my life and I found myself becoming as enthusiastic as Bill, Dr. Mears and other students were, and as eager as they were to share Christ with others.

While Dr. Mears and Vonette talked, I paced back and forth outside the cottage, praying. Time dragged—fifteen minutes, half an hour. Suddenly the door burst open and Vonette came bounding into my arms. There were tears on her cheeks and an indescribable look of joy on her face. She did not need to say a word. I knew what had happened, and tears of gratitude filled my eyes, too.

Soon after the purchase of Arrowhead Springs, Dr. Mears came to see the property and participated in our first institute by offering a special prayer of dedication to the Lord for us and for Arrowhead Springs. This was especially meaningful to us because of the important role which she had played in our personal lives and in the ministry of Campus Crusade for Christ. Since Vonette and I had shared her home in Bel-Air for ten years, both as our own home and as a headquarters and meeting place for our campus ministry at UCLA, and since she was now prepared to retire from her ministry with the First Presbyterian Church of Hollywood as director of Christian education, we invited her to come to live with us at Arrowhead Springs. This she was prayerfully considering when the Lord chose to take her home—a great loss to us and to the cause of Christ, yet we know that He does all things well and our confidence is in Him. Multitudes from around the world have been spiritually blessed and benefited, even as we have been, by the great ministry of Henrietta Mears.

The miracle of UCLA continued. One of the highlights of my experience there was the day that Bob and Barbara Davenport handed me a little gift-wrapped box. Upon opening it, I discovered a beautiful watch with an alarm on it. I was very pleased, but could not understand why they were giving me such an expensive gift. Then Bob told me to turn the watch over and read the inscription on the back. It read: "Bob Davenport, Warner Award, 1955, to Bill, from Bob and Barbara."

I looked at Bob in amazement because this meant that he was giving me his most coveted award, one of the most prized awards, apart from the Heisman trophy that an athlete on the West Coast can receive. I said, "Bob, I can't accept it. This is something that you should save for yourself or give to your son."

But he insisted that because God had used Vonette and me in helping him and Barbara come to know Christ in a vital way, they wanted me to have the watch as an expression of their gratitude and love. You can well imagine how moved I was. In fact, I did what I always do when my heart is filled with joy and gratitude and I have no words to express it: I suggested that we pray. We all knelt together and prayed that as I traveled around the country God would use Bob's watch as a means of telling others the good news of our Savior. God has answered that prayer many times.

For example, a few days later I was on another great campus where the assistant football coach, not knowing that I had had any personal contact with Bob Davenport, told me of a moving experience he had had only a few days before while attending the Pop Warner banquet at Stanford. He said that the young man who had received the award was one of the most remarkable athletes he had ever known. Coaches and sports writers agreed that he was the most deserving athlete ever to receive the award. (Here I sat in this coach's office wearing the very award Bob had received!) He continued, saying that upon receipt of the watch Davenport had given the most inspiring speech that he had ever heard. He was referring to Bob's personal testimony of his faith in Christ. I was very conscious of my unworthiness to wear the award, and sat there debating whether or not to show the watch to this coach. Finally, I pulled it off and handed it to him. He looked at me in disbelief, as though I surely must be mistaken. I could almost read his mind, as he must have wondered if I had stolen the watch! And then he shook his head in amazement, looking at me through tear-filled eyes. He realized that Bob Davenport's testimony was more than words. The most important thing in Bob's life was not awards, but Christ.

Later, as I was visiting Michigan State University, I met a junior who was a star football player and who had won all-American honors in both high school and junior college in California. The first thing the young man asked me was, "Do you know Bob Davenport?"

I assured him that I did, and asked if he knew Bob.

"No," he replied, "but I have been one of his admirers for many years."

Bob Davenport had once spoken in his high school assembly, he explained, and had given such an inspiring and challenging talk that it had made a lasting impact on the athlete before me. Knowing that Bob never spoke unless he could give his witness for Christ, I asked this young man if Bob had spoken of his faith in Christ, and he said he had. Then I pulled off the watch Bob had given me, and the young man looked at it in wide-eyed amazement. After explaining why Bob had given it to me, I asked him if he had made the wonderful discovery of knowing Christ personally. He said, "No, I have gone to church almost every Sunday since I heard Bob Davenport speak in my high school assembly some years ago but I have not yet made this decision. I don't know how."

Very quickly I explained how he could know Christ personally, and as we knelt together he prayed to commit his life to Christ. All of this happened in a matter of minutes, because God had already prepared his heart and had again used Bob Davenport's watch in answer to our prayer.

Another story indicates how strong a witness for Christ Bob Davenport gave. It involves Don Shinnick, another UCLA all-American and later all-pro with the Baltimore Colts. Don was a great high school athlete with unusual promise. In bringing Don to UCLA, the coaches had led him to expect that he would become one of the school's most outstanding linebackers. But, much to his disappointment, he found that another young man already occupied his position. That young man's name was Bob Davenport. No bad spirit developed between these two, however. Shinnick was so impressed with Davenport and his witness for Christ that he and Bob became good friends. In fact, Davenport played an important role in bringing Don to commit his life to Christ.

For three years Don played second string to Davenport and saw very little action, though he was recognized as a first-rate linebacker himself. Then, Bob began to have difficulty with his knees. He had received serious injuries in the past and sometimes his trick knees gave him difficulty. One day he was experiencing such excruciating pain that he was in danger of having to miss the next Saturday's important game. To my amazement Don Shinnick, who by this time had made a full commitment to Christ and was excited about living all out for the Lord Jesus, came to our home and asked me to pray for Bobby. As we knelt together, he said, "I want you to pray that God will strengthen Bobby's knees, so that he will be able to play in Saturday's game." This was especially meaningful to me because had Bob not been able to play, Shinnick would have had a chance to show his ability. As it turned out, Davenport did play brilliantly, and no one was cheering him more enthusiastically than a second stringer on the bench. That's the spirit that exists when Christians are on the same team.

5

Moving Out

From UCLA our training headquarters was moved to Minnesota. In the fall of 1956 a long-distance call came from Mound, Minnesota, from Bill Greig, chairman of the Midwest Keswick. He wondered if Campus Crusade for Christ would be interested in receiving a gift of a five-acre tract of land in Mound, Minnesota, on the shore of beautiful Lake Minnetonka. Since his group could no longer use the property, they were looking for an organization that would utilize it effectively for the glory of God. "Come out and look it over," Bill said. "If it fits your needs, it's yours."

I expressed gratefulness for the offer, but only when I saw the site did I fully appreciate the gift. Though the buildings were old and mostly run down and there was only a rough foundation for a new chapel-dormitory building, the place offered great promise. It was a breathtakingly beautiful site. I knew it would be ideal for a training center for our staff and students, so we gratefully accepted title to it. In the summer of 1957 we completed a beautiful chapel and dormitory combination which, together with existing facilities which we had also remodeled, enabled us to train approximately 150 people at one time.

That first summer we had that number and more. We also had our troubles trying to get the buildings completed. Carpenters, masons and electricians were everywhere. The staff and local volunteers were still painting and building partitions in the dormitories when the students arrived. As a matter of fact, the students joined with the staff in finishing the job. There were problems, too, more than I care to remember. But even these problems served to draw us closer together, so great was the challenge and excitement of moving into our beautiful new training center.

Many heart-warming experiences took place at Mound as hundreds of students dedicated their lives to helping fulfil the Great Commission in this generation. But it was at UCLA that all of us learned an important lesson. We found that we, teachers and pupils alike, were not only learning new techniques each year but were also learning and discovering depths of God's love and facets of His truth we had never known before.

One of our speakers for staff training that summer was a Christian layman who was an outstanding sales consultant, a man who had taught thousands of salesmen how to sell. One of the main points of one of his addresses was that to be a successful salesman a man must have a pitch. In other words, a man who is a good automobile salesman tells every potential customer basically the same things, and the better he communicates, the more successful he is as a salesman. But the danger, he explained, is that when a man becomes weary of hearing himself make the same presentation, he develops presentation fatigue. When this happens, he often changes the message and loses his effectiveness.

He compared the witnessing Christian to the secular salesman. To be effective in our ministry for Christ we must have, in his words, "a spiritual pitch." He illustrated his remarks by telling how several well-known Christians had their own special pitch. He spoke of a famous minister who always said basically the same thing; no matter what the problem, his emphasis was the same. He told of a woman, an outstanding Christian leader, who always prescribed the same spiritual solution for whatever problem was presented. He cited successful evangelists who always preach the same basic message under different titles. Then he zeroed in on me, and said, "Bill Bright, who works with students and professors and outstanding business executives, as well as with men on Skid Row, thinks that he has a special message for each of them, but the fact of the matter is, though I have never heard him speak or counsel, I would be willing to wager that he has only one pitch. Basically, he tells them all the same thing." To say that I objected to such a suggestion is to put it mildly. The very thought that a man needed to resort to what I considered Madison Avenue techniques to do the spiritual work of God was repugnant and offensive to me.

The longer he spoke, the more distressed I became. I resented anyone suggesting that I or anyone else who truly desired to serve the Lord had to depend on gimmicks, or that we were not led of the Spirit in such a way that the Holy Spirit was able to be original through us to the various individuals with whom we worked, according to their various needs. Furthermore, I resented his using me as an example before the rest of the staff. So, when it was all over and I was licking my wounds (the most serious of which was a lacerated ego) I began to reflect on exactly what I shared with the various ones with whom I worked, young or old, management or labor, Episcopalian or Baptist, students or professors, or the men in jails or on Skid Row. That afternoon I wrote down my basic presentation and, to my amazement, my friend was right. I had been sharing basically the same thing with everyone, without realizing it.

What I wrote that afternoon (and later polished) is now known as "God's Plan for Your Life." I asked each staff member to memorize it. We all began to share this presentation in personal interviews and in various team meetings on the college campus. Because of this one presentation alone, our ministry was multiplied a hundredfold during the next year.

For those who are not familiar with "God's Plan," I should explain that it is a positive, twenty-minute presentation of the claims of Christ: who He is, why He came and how man can know Him personally. It does not contain any startling new truths. It is a simple statement of the gospel. However, God has used its presentation by our staff, in the power and control of the Holy Spirit, to draw countless thousands more to Himself.

"God's Plan" was our first written how-to material. The how-to approach is one of the most needed and most revolutionary concepts I have ever encountered. There has been a tendency in certain academic and theological circles to play down the simple approach to living the Christian life and sharing our faith with others. "Such an approach is simplistic and anti-intellectual," some have said. It required several years and considerable front-line spiritual combat experience in my work with students, professors and laymen, for certain great concepts to begin to come into focus in a revolutionary way. The longer I worked with the intelligentsia the more I realized the necessity of developing simple how-to's for the Christian life.

I personally became a Christian while operating my own business, which I had worked day and night to start and build. Soon after becoming a Christian, I found that I was spending most of my time sharing Christ. But I needed to know more about Him. For the next five years, from 1946 to 1951, I studied under some of the greatest scholars of the Christian world, to whom I shall always be indebted. I learned many things about the Christian life. But like many other seminarians—and other Christians, for that matter—I was unable to put together the pieces of the spiritual jigsaw puzzle. I did not know the how-to of the Christian life.

Now, we have found that the twentieth century counterpart of "the masses who heard Jesus gladly" when He spoke in a language they understood, responds with great joy and enthusiasm to our presentation of certain how-to's or "transferable concepts" that relate to the Christian life and witness of the believer. For example, the Four Spiritual Laws presentation, which is the distilled essence of God's Plan and of the gospel, has been used by thousands of Christians around the world. At last count an estimated twenty-five million copies in booklet form had been distributed, in most of the major languages of the world. There is no doubt that tens, if not hundreds, of thousands of men and women have been introduced to Christ through this presentation of the gospel. I know of at least 2,000 individuals who in one afternoon, through the use of the Four Spiritual Laws by our staff and students here in Southern California, prayed to receive Christ.

Though we had found the twenty-minute presentation of God's Plan to be extremely effective, we realized that we needed a much shorter version of the gospel in order to communicate quickly, clearly and simply to those whose hearts were already prepared to receive Christ. I prepared a condensed outline of God's Plan, complete with Scripture verses and diagrams, and asked the staff to memorize it. For several years we wrote it out as we were sharing Christ in a witnessing experience. Then, as more and more people became involved in the training program of Campus Crusade for Christ, it became apparent that we needed to make the Four Spiritual Laws presentation available in printed form to insure faithfulness to the content and uniformity of presentation. Thus, the booklet was born.

As the name suggests, there are four basic truths to the Four Spiritual Laws: (1) God *loves* you and has a wonderful *plan* for your life. (2) Man is *sinful* and *separated* from God, thus he cannot know and experience God's love and plan for his life. (3) Jesus Christ is God's *only* provision for man's sin. Through Him you can know and experience God's love and plan for your life. (4) We must individually *receive* Jesus Christ as Savior and Lord; then we can know and experience God's love and plan for our lives.

I remember that this was not the way we had expressed the first law in the original draft, but this change was made just before we went to press. I had done my final editing and had left Vonette and the girls to finish the typing. As I had been traveling a great deal and it was quite late, I had gone upstairs to bed. In fact, I was in bed, just at the point of going to sleep, when suddenly there came clear as a bell to my conscious mind the fact that there was something wrong about starting the Four Laws on the negative note of man's sinfulness. Why not start where God starts, with His love? I had been drawn to Christ originally because I was overwhelmed with God's love. The love of God had been the basis of my presentation of the gospel ever since I had become a Christian. I wanted everyone to know how much God loves him and that God has a wonderful plan for the life of everyone who will accept His plan. I felt that few people would say "no" to Christ if they truly understood how much He loves them and how great is His concern for them.

So I got out of bed, went to the head of the stairs and called down to Vonette and the girls to revise the presentation so that the first law would be, "God loves you and has a wonderful plan for your life," instead of "You are a sinner and separated from God." We moved the statement of the fact of man's sin and separation from God, making it Law Two. Thus, the Four Spiritual Laws started with the positive note of God's love. There were other minor revisions, but this was the basic one.

Sometime later, one of the girls said to me, "I was so distressed over your change in the presentation that I wept that night. I was afraid that you were beginning to dilute the gospel and that you were no longer faithful to the Lord, because you placed such a

46

strong emphasis on the love of God rather than on man's sin. Now, in retrospect, I realize of course that this is one of the greatest things that has ever happened to the Campus Crusade for Christ ministry." Now literally millions of people all over the world are being told, through the presentation of the Four Spiritual Laws, that God loves them and has a wonderful plan for their lives. Can you think of any more exciting, wonderful message than this to proclaim to the world?

Each of these four laws is illustrated by portions of Scripture and diagrams. We have discovered that most people believe the first three laws. However, many people need counsel and assistance in regard to the fourth law. Though most people believe that Jesus Christ is the Son of God and realize their need of Him as Savior, they do not know what to do about it. So, the simple presentation of the Four Spiritual Laws helps the honest inquirers, which most people are, to know what to do.

This little booklet is so simple that one marvels at its effectiveness. I could tell you hundreds of stories—thrilling stories—of how God has used it to reach people who have not responded to previous presentations. I think, for example, of an assistant minister whose senior pastor had come to Arrowhead Springs for training. The senior pastor was very excited about the Four Spiritual Laws presentation. He went back to share his enthusiasm with his church and with his assistant minister. The assistant minister was turned off by the *Four Spiritual Laws* booklet. He had a dislike for tracts, and this looked like just another tract to him. He tossed the booklet aside on his desk. A few days later a city official, a woman, came by to inspect the facilities of the church plant. As the woman was about to leave, following the inspection tour, it suddenly occurred to the man that he had not talked to her about Christ. He looked around quickly and the only thing he saw was this little *Four Spiritual Laws* booklet, which he had tossed aside in disgust some days previously and had not bothered to read. He reached for the booklet to give it to her, as the pastor had suggested, thinking it certainly would not do her any harm. "Read this," he said, meaning that she should read it when she got home. She misunderstood, however, and began to read it aloud in his presence. She read every word, and by the time she got through Laws 1, 2, and 3 and began to read Law 4, tears were streaming down her cheeks. She came to the prayer and prayed aloud, leading *herself* to Christ. By this time the assistant was so overwhelmed that he vowed to go to Arrowhead Springs and to find out for himself how he could use the Four Spiritual Laws. He decided that it was far more effective than anything or any other method he had ever employed.

A missionary friend in Japan shared a heartwarming experience of his use of the *Four Spiritual Laws*. There was a man who was greatly admired in his hometown, though he was not a Christian. In fact, he was known as the town atheist. Whenever there was any kind of evangelistic meeting in his city, the pastors, evangelists, and laymen would call on him but he would never respond. My missionary friend, whose parents had been befriended by this man, felt indebted to him and was concerned for his soul. After obtaining a *Four Spiritual Laws* booklet, the missionary decided to call on his friend and read it to him. As he finished reading he asked, "Does this make sense?" The atheist replied in the affirmative.

"Is there anything that would keep you from receiving Christ?"

"No," was the reply.

The two men knelt together and prayed and the atheist invited Jesus into his life. When they arose my friend was rejoicing with the man, who then stunned him with this question, "Chuck, is this what you and all the other Christian leaders have been trying to tell me for years?"

When my missionary friend nodded, the man continued, "Well, why didn't you tell me? Any man would be a fool not to receive Christ if he really understood what is involved." Obviously, others had been trying to communicate the gospel, but had been unsuccessful. The *Four Spiritual Laws* presentation of the gospel had cut right through the barrier of skepticism and indifference so that the professing atheist got the message. We have found that the average person does not need to be convinced that he should become a Christian; he needs, rather, to be told *how* to become a Christian. I should hasten to explain that it is the Holy Spirit who uses this presentation as He empowers the one giving the witness and enlightens the one who hears and responds.

There is no magic in the *Four Spiritual Laws* booklet. God blesses its use because it contains the distilled essence of the gospel, especially when it is used by men who are controlled and empowered by the Holy Spirit.

48

The second most important how-to in our training explains how to be filled, controlled and empowered by the Holy Spirit. Like many other sincere seekers after the "deep things of God" I had sought for many years to understand the person and work of the Holy Spirit. For many days at a time I fasted and prayed in my attempt to discover new depths of meaning in my Christian experience. Though I had on numerous occasions enjoyed a wonderful fellowship with the Lord and even had several experiences when I knew the Holy Spirit had touched my life, and used me, I knew nothing of how to appropriate the fullness and power of the Holy Spirit by faith, nor of how to live under His control. I made a special study of the Person and work of the Holy Spirit which included almost every book on the subject I could lay my hands on. I was hungry for all that God had for me. I longed to be a man of God whatever the cost and knew that this desire could be fulfilled only through the ministry of the Holy Spirit in my life.

One summer in the early years of the Campus Crusade for Christ ministry, Vonette and I were invited to spend a few days in the Newport Beach home of Dr. and Mrs. Charles Fuller. Dr. Fuller, a famous evangelist, conducted the "Old Fashioned Revival Hour" on the radio, and was the founder of Fuller Theological Seminary. He and his family were very dear to us and we accepted the invitation gratefully. Vonette and I were both very tired. Our schedule had been extremely busy and crowded, with no vacation for several years, and we could think of nothing more inviting than having a few days to sleep, lie in the sun and swim in the ocean. The midnight hour had come and gone by the time we had arrived and unpacked. Some time near one o'clock in the morning we wearily climbed into bed and fully expected to be asleep by the time the light was out.

But God had other plans. As I turned over to go to sleep, I found my mind flooded with truths concerning the Holy Spirit. Fearful that I might forget them if I didn't write them down, I got up for pencil and paper and found several shirt boards. After filling the shirt boards, I found some brown wrapping paper and continued to write furiously. That night God gave me the truths concerning the Person and work of the Holy Spirit that have been basic to the ministry of Campus Crusade for Christ through the years. This material has now been incorporated into our Bible study course, *Ten Basic Steps toward Christian Maturity,* which is being used by many churches and various Christian organizations around the world. This basic and revolutionary concept of how to be filled with the Holy Spirit has been condensed into a small booklet comparable to the Four Spiritual Laws presentation and is entitled, "Have You Made the Wonderful Discovery of the Spirit-filled Life?" This Holy Spirit booklet is being used by many thousands of Christians all over the world to help lead carnal Christians into an abundant and fruitful life in the Spirit as well as to help new Christians understand their spiritual heritage in Christ. Like the Four Laws presentation, this brief presentation of the ministry of the Holy Spirit is having revolutionary results.

6

Story of a Miracle

By 1960 our staff numbered 109 and we were serving Christ on forty campuses in fifteen states. Furthermore, we had established ourselves in Korea and Pakistan. We had also begun a weekly radio broadcast which was carried on several local stations without any cost to Campus Crusade for Christ.

It had long since become obvious that we had outgrown our facilities at Mound, Minnesota, and we had begun to intensify our search for a solution to our expansion problem. We knew that we must either build or purchase larger facilities in the Lake Minnetonka region, or find more adequate facilities elsewhere across the nation. It was then that word came from a long-time friend George Rowan, president of the R. A. Rowan Company in Los Angeles, that the famous Arrowhead Springs Hotel and Spa was for sale at "a greatly reduced price." All of which brings me to the experience I related in the beginning of this book.

I came away from that memorable visit to Arrowhead Springs convinced that Campus Crusade for Christ would one day occupy these beautiful facilities. The impression that God wanted this facility for Campus Crusade was so real that almost every day I found myself expecting a telephone call from some person saying that he had heard about our interest in Arrowhead Springs and that he would purchase it for us. I felt certain the Lord did not want me to write letters inviting people to invest, believing instead that God had a plan already working. Vonette and I, and other members of the staff of Campus Crusade for Christ, purposely limited our concern to prayer. For fourteen months we prayed that if God wanted us to have Arrowhead Springs, He would provide the funds in some supernatural or unusual way.

Increasingly I knew that God wanted us to move to Arrowhead Springs, though there was no tangible evidence of that fact. That is not to say that my faith never wavered. Sometimes the thought came, "What if someone else buys the property?" Then deep down in my heart I knew that it would eventually be ours. Still I frequently prayed that He would not let us have Arrowhead Springs unless it was His perfect will for us. I well knew that to become involved in raising money for such a big project could well sabotage our spiritual ministry and destroy Campus Crusade for Christ in the process.

While we were praying we were also working. Among other things we did a feasibility study of the property, a careful cost analysis of what was involved in operating the grounds, figuring the cost for maintenance and repairs and the operation of the various facilities. After several weeks of careful analysis, various factors convinced us that if money could be raised for the capital investment, we could carry the load and operate in the black from almost the very beginning. The factors included such items as our office rental in Los Angeles, our expenses for the various training conference grounds which we rented from time to time, and the fact that the headquarters staff would be living on the Arrowhead Springs campus, and thus would pay rent there. Our conviction was strengthened by a dedicated staff willing to work long hours and without thought of personal remuneration or glory.

Then it happened. The telephone rang. Henry Hanson, the father of two students who had been influenced for Christ through our ministry was on the line. Through him negotiations were begun with the owner, Benjamin Swig. Mr. Swig proved to be most cooperative, helpful and generous during the period of negotiation. Though we had not asked for financial help during the fourteen months of waiting and praying, I now felt, after my conversation with Mr. Swig, that the Lord wanted me to share this opportunity with some of my close friends. Among those who came to look over the property and to interact with me were Dean Griffith, J. D. Forney, Gerri Von Frellick, Lawson Ridgeway, Clinton McKinnon, John McGill, Sterling Hogan, Henry Hanson, Guy Martin, Elmer

52

and Warren Bradley, George Rowan and Arlis Priest. These men were all outstandingly successful men, dedicated to Christ and vitally interested in the ministry of Campus Crusade. Many of our close friends, however, were far from being of one mind concerning the wisdom of making the purchase. Some were convinced that it would be foolhardy and a poor stewardship of the Lord's money to purchase the property, while others believed that Campus Crusade needed training facilities such as Arrowhead Springs would supply. On the basis of God's previous blessing on the ministry, this was another opportunity for us to trust Him for even greater things. A few individuals supported their convictions with offers to help make the down payment.

After careful and prayerful consideration of loans and gifts, the board of directors, acting upon the advice of these men who were interested in helping us, advised us to make an offer to Mr. Swig. The offer was a $15,000 deposit toward a $2 million purchase price, with an additional $130,000 to be paid within thirty days after we signed the contract. Amazingly, the offer was accepted. With an empty bank book we were buying a $2 million property! It was the greatest act of faith I had ever seen or in which I had ever had a part. We borrowed the $15,000 needed for the deposit and on the weekend of December 1, 1962, Campus Crusade for Christ International moved from its Westwood, Los Angeles, office to Arrowhead Springs.

We still did not have the necessary $130,000 for the next payment but several friends had agreed to help and, interpreting this as God's will, we took the first step by advancing the $15,000 as a deposit. Thirty days later at the last minute an additional $130,000 had been given by interested friends and I dashed off to San Francisco to see Mr. Swig and make the payment to consummate the purchase. The monthly payment schedule was a very stiff one and there followed a series of financial cliff-hanging experiences that forced us to depend wholly upon the Lord. Every move financially was a precarious one for months—indeed, for the first several years. God used the faith, work, and prayer of a dedicated staff to make Arrowhead Springs possible.

From the start, God blessed and used the headquarters in a spiritual way that surpassed all our expectations. Hundreds of young men and women, and adults as well, came to Arrowhead

Springs for training that first year, and their lives were transformed. We had the assurance that the day would come when God would send a thousand people per week to Arrowhead Springs for training. Already that goal has been exceeded for several months each year with as many as 1,500 in attendance for several weeks at a time.

The decision to acquire Arrowhead Springs as our international headquarters and institute for evangelism for the world-wide ministry was to be one of the most significant ones that we had ever made. When Arlis Priest, outstanding Phoenix businessman, visited Arrowhead Springs prior to our purchase, he volunteered, "If God should make this property available to you, I would like to give my services for one year without salary to help you get the headquarters operating efficiently." His life had been greatly affected in one of our day-long institutes in Phoenix, and this was his way of thanking us. Imagine his surprise a few weeks later when I took him up on the offer. "How soon can you come?" I asked over the phone. "We are now ready to move into the Arrowhead Springs campus, and we need a manager."

"I'll call you back later today and give you an answer," he said. Within a matter of days, he was with us; and God used him mightily to help organize and get the long-closed facilities operating efficiently. I do not know how we would have done it without him and his lovely wife, Nadine, who was not only a great help herself, but was willing for Arlis to work day and night to help us get into operation. The dedication of the entire headquarters staff was a joy to behold. A normal day ran ten, twelve, fifteen hours—all with a joyful spirit.

May 17, 1963, found several hundred friends of Campus Crusade for Christ gathered for our dedication of Arrowhead Springs as our international headquarters and Institute for Evangelism. Dr. Walter Judd brought the dedication address. The mayor and many outstanding local officials were present. The mayor stated, "The finest thing that has ever happened to the city of San Bernardino is the coming of Campus Crusade for Christ to Arrowhead Springs." Dr. Judd brought one of his characteristically inspiring and challenging messages. Participating in the program were Dr. Bob Pierce, president of World Vision; Dr. Dick Hillis, president of Overseas Crusade; Armin Gesswein, director of Pastors' Revival Fellowship;

Dr. Walter Smith, vice-president of the Billy Graham Evangelistic Association; Dr. Carlton Booth, professor of Evangelism, Fuller Theological Seminary; Dr. Roger Voskyle, president of Westmont College; and Dr. John MacArthur, leading evangelist and radio pastor.

A very interesting, and I believe symbolic, occurrence took place that day during the very hour of the dedication. Our good friend, George Rowan, had started drilling for a steam well on the property twenty-seven days previously and the bit had reached a depth of 500 feet. Steam has great value for generating electricity and, if discovered, would be very valuable to Campus Crusade for Christ. To move the drilling rig that night from Arrowhead Springs to an urgent assignment in Nevada, they were rushing to drill as deep as possible that day before tearing down the rig. They had not yet struck any sign of steam or any large vein of water, and it looked doubtful that anything would come of his drilling venture. Because of the noise the drilling was stopped while the dedication program was in progress. During the program, however, the water pressure broke through the undrilled porous granite and began to flow down the mountainside!

In the meantime, not knowing of this event, after Dr. Judd's message, I closed with a prayer asking God that there might *flow* from this center of training a great spiritual blessing that would engulf the world through the tens of thousands of men and women trained here in the ministry of evangelism and proclaiming near and far the good news of God's love and forgiveness in Christ everywhere. Shortly after the benediction George Rowan came running back from the well, out of breath. "We hit an ocean of hot water," he exclaimed. "When?" I asked. "About five minutes ago." We checked the time; it was the exact time I had prayed. We interpreted this as being symbolic of what God was going to do spiritually. Just as this great artesian well was to thrust forth hundreds of gallons of hot water per minute, so was God to send forth His blessing from Arrowhead Springs to the far reaches of the world.

Among those present for the dedication were Elmer Bradley, a leading businessman and subsequently mayor of Tempe, Arizona, and his wife, Ellen. Elmer was present for our first meeting at the time we were making the decision to purchase Arrowhead Springs.

Spontaneously, knowing of our need for additional finances, Elmer and Ellen volunteered to memorialize one of the 130 rooms in the hotel for $15,000. This was the beginning of our program to memorialize rooms at Arrowhead Springs and at Chula Vista, our Latin American Institute of Evangelism and training center.

Also present at the dedication service that day were Mr. and Mrs. Guy F. Atkinson. Mr. Atkinson was one of the world's leading builders of roads, dams, bridges and other multimillion-dollar construction projects. He was then eighty-nine years of age—sharp, alert, and very astute. He inquired what we planned to do with the property and asked more questions about the ministry of Campus Crusade for Christ at Arrowhead Springs than any group of people had ever asked me in its history. Some months later he again expressed interest in helping; but before he did anything he wanted to send his attorney to look over our financial records and our corporation structure, including the bylaws. This we were very happy for him to do. After several days of careful study of the organizational structure and policies and financial records by himself and his attorney. Mr. Atkinson announced that he would like to give $300,000 if we would raise the balance of the then $1,570,000 still due on the $2,000,000 purchase. Of course, this was an exciting challenge. He gave us exactly one year to raise that amount, and we set forth with great enthusiasm and determination to raise a sum so great that I could hardly even comprehend the amount. It might as well have been a billion dollars. Yet, we were confident that God would help us.

With the passing of the months, however, it seemed that we were not going to be able to reach our goal of $1,570,000 to qualify for Mr. Atkinson's $300,000 pledge. In spite of the additional challenge that was offered when Mr. Swig agreed to discount $100,000 from the balance due, and the additional savings of $120,000 in interest, which, with Mr. Atkinson's pledge of $300,000, would mean a total gift and savings of $520,000, we became aware that we were faced with an impossible task. We asked Mr. Atkinson if he would still be willing to pledge his $300,000 if we raised part of the balance by selling some of the land. He agreed to this with the understanding that we would not sell more than 400 acres of our 1,735-acre total.

Arlis Priest and I had interested a group of twenty laymen in the idea of purchasing $1,000,000 dollars worth of our land from us. It was estimated that by selling approximately 400 acres we could raise that amount. When Mr. Atkinson agreed that we could sell a million dollars worth of land and raise the balance through gifts, we took new courage and approached the deadline of June 30, 1965, with confidence. In the meantime Arlis Priest and Howard Ball, a member of our lay staff, were devoting considerable time to contacting potential contributors in an attempt to raise the balance. In spite of the additional encouragement, we found that we would still fall short of the amount needed. I had made a commitment to the Lord that I would not allow Arrowhead Springs or the raising of funds to interfere with my spiritual ministry or the ministries of any of our campus staff. In fact, none of the field staff were ever asked to become involved in raising funds at any time because we felt that it was a tangible expression of our trust in the Lord to put our spiritual ministry first. We were confident that if we sought first the kingdom of God, the Lord would meet our financial needs.

Thus, in the last week prior to the deadline, I found myself speaking at very important conferences several times a day and unable to make any significant contribution to the raising of funds. Dr. V. Raymond Edman, president of Wheaton College, came to speak for an educators' conference at the same time a student conference was in session. He shared with Vonette and me a very meaningful verse that God had given him that morning while he was praying for our needs. The verse was especially appropriate: ". . . he that putteth his trust in me shall possess the land, and shall inherit my holy mountain." [1] We will always be grateful to Dr. Edman for his special concern and prayers for us during those urgent days of crises, as well as for the great ministry of his life and witness with us.

On the evening of the deadline, I met with Arlis just before I was to bring a message to the conference then in session. He informed me that we still needed $33,000 and that every possible source of revenue had been exhausted. There was nothing more, humanly speaking, that we could do. After the completion of my message about 9 o'clock in the evening, I inquired again as to our progress; and, though several members of the staff were gathering and praying, working, and hoping, the situation remained unchanged. I assumed that there was nothing more that I could do personally so I went to our cottage on the campus, too weary to give further thought to the matter.

I was dressing for bed when Vonette returned with the boys from a youth meeting. "All of the money must be in or you would not be going to bed," she said.

I told her that that was not the case, adding, "I've done all I know to do. I will have to leave the rest in the Lord's hands."

"Honey, I have never seen you give up so easily before," Vonette said.

"If the miracle is going to happen, the Lord will have to do it right away," I replied.

It was then about 10 P.M. and we had two hours to go before the deadline. What happened in the next two hours involved a gain or loss of $520,000. We had been praying for months, but as Vonette and I now knelt with our two sons Zachary and Bradley, we prayed with a new urgency. I prayed first, then Vonette and then Zach. But it was Brad's prayer that I remember. He was only seven years old but he spoke to the heart of the matter, "Lord, we need this money and we ask You to send it right away."

After all of us had prayed and the boys had gone to bed, I reached for my Bible, to read before turning out the light. As I did so I saw a scrap of paper I had brought home from my office. It had memos on both sides. I had read only one side; now I saw the other side. There was a telephone number on it. Gerri Von Frellick had called me the day before and had asked me to call him back. I had failed to get the message. I checked my watch and by now it was 10:30, which meant that it was about 11:30 P.M. at his home in Denver, Colorado. I debated whether I should return his call at such a late hour. "Maybe Gerri has some suggestion to make about contributions," Vonette suggested. I finally decided to call him even though it was very late. He answered the phone sleepily and I apologized for waking him up. "How are you getting along with your fund-raising campaign?" he asked.

I told him that we had an hour and thirty minutes to go and still lacked $33,000. He said that he wanted to send us $5,000 if it would help us meet our goal and would send it the next morning. Gerri had already given generously when we first moved to Arrowhead Springs. Now he was giving again. This, of course, was encouraging and yet at that point I did not think that $5,000 was going to make much difference, but I thanked him warmly and hung up. "You were right, Vonette," I said. "He did have some money for us. Now we need only $28,000."

Suddenly it occurred to me that a month or so before, a businessman in Arizona had given us a piece of property not far from Denver, for which we had been offered $17,000 by a local attorney. If he would pay us $20,000 for the property, that would reduce the balance to only $8,000 and there was still a possibility that we could meet that amount. The more I thought about it the more excited I became so I placed a call to the attorney in Colorado, who I realized was also probably in bed asleep. Shortly, the attorney was on the line. I reminded him that a month ago he had offered $17,000 for the property and that we would be willing because of a particular need to take $22,000 for it. He countered with $18,000 and said he would wire it the next morning. I accepted his offer. Now we were within $10,000 of our goal.

I called the switchboard at the hotel and reported the good news. I heard a big cheer when staff and friends learned we were within sight of our goal.

In the meantime members of our staff were gathered in the lobby of the hotel, praying and giving generously of their own limited funds—not because they were asked, but because they were impressed by the Lord to do so. Arlis Priest recalls that dramatic evening: "It was getting late. Nadine and I were both in bed when some of the staff began to knock at our door. This happened several times. Each time some staffer would hand me an envelope with money in it. The first few I looked at were $25, $100 and $150. A peace came over me for I knew God was doing something special. These dedicated staff who had hardly enough money to live on were giving the widow's mite."

With less than thirty minutes before the deadline we had $10,000 more to raise. We were all getting increasingly excited. Surely God was going to answer our need!

When Dr. Walter Judd, who had come to Arrowhead Springs to speak at one of our conferences, returned from speaking at a local medical association meeting, he inquired as to the progress of the fund-raising campaign and was informed that we were close to both our goal and the deadline. Now it was about fifteen minutes until midnight. "Have Bill call me," he told the switchboard operator.

When I called he said that he would like to give the last $5,000 and I should call him back if his money was needed. In the meantime Vonette (her mind was working overtime) reminded me that Al Curtis, at my request, had put aside some months previously a $5,000 gift from Mr. Atkinson, money which had been given to be used wherever we felt it was most needed. (I had asked Al Curtis to assume responsibility for managing the Arrowhead Springs property when Arlis Priest was assigned to another responsibility as my personal assistant.) We had agreed then that the money should be held for this very deadline in case of need. Yet, at the moment I had temporarily forgotten about it. I called Al, who had just returned from Los Angeles and a futile attempt to raise funds, and he verified the fact that we had $5,000. "Get it ready," I told him.

This meant that we needed only Dr. Judd's gift of $5,000. At two minutes till midnight and our deadline I called him to make sure that I had understood his offer. "I will pledge that amount," he repeated, and a minute later I called the hotel lobby and an anxious, waiting staff to announce that God had worked another miracle.

By this time Vonette and I and the members of the staff were so excited and filled with gratitude to the Lord that we decided to meet immediately in the International Theater to thank Him for this miracle. We quickly dressed and rushed to the hotel. The International Theater was packed to overflowing with grateful staff and friends. For the next couple of hours we sang and worshiped the Lord. The office girls, some of them with their hair in rollers, in pajamas and housecoats; faculty, who were there for an educators' conference; and other workers, all came together. It was a beautiful experience, one of the highlights of my spiritual life. Never have I heard the doxology sung with such vigor. Never did the lyrics, "Praise God from whom all blessings flow . . ." hold so much meaning.

7

The Trial of Faith

The good news of what God had done had to be told. I could hardly wait to inform all of our friends of the miracle God had performed, and soon a letter was dispatched to thousands on our mailing list and to personal friends and supporters, telling them that the deadline had been met and that Campus Crusade for Christ had been able to pay off the total indebtedness against the Arrowhead Springs property. In part I wrote:

Rejoice and give thanks to the Lord with us. The miracle has happened! God has answered prayer! Exactly two minutes before the June 30 deadline, at 11:58 P.M., the goal of $1,570,000 was reached which qualified us for a $300,000 pledge, and the future of Arrowhead Springs as our International Headquarters and International Institute of Evangelism was assured (sale of the land involved in the transaction is to be consummated in approximately sixty days).

The details of how it happened are far more dramatic than words could ever describe. We had prayed that God would provide the needed finances in such a way that the end result would cause all men to acknowledge His supernatural provision and that all honor, glory and praise would go to Him. God has answered this prayer, for no man could have planned the final days prior to the deadline as exciting, dramatic and fruitful as He had arranged them. . . .

The letter was sent, and calls and letters of congratulations came back from all over the country.

But the story was not ended. Ten days later the appraisers announced that the acreage required for the one million dollar sale of the property was approximately 120 acres more than we had thought would be needed. The twenty friends who had agreed to purchase the land were going to borrow the $1,000,000 from an insurance company, purchase the land and later sell or develop it and give any profits to Campus Crusade for Christ. but to borrow that amount it was necessary for the value of the land to be at least double the amount of the loan, which meant that $2,000,000 worth of land had to be made available to the men who were making the purchase for them to secure a $1,000,000 loan.

When I informed Mr. Atkinson of these developments, he was disturbed. He said he wanted to see me immediately. When he arrived from his La Canada home, he reminded me, as we sat in my office, that his original agreement called for our raising in contributions and pledges the entire amount of $1,570,000 to match his contribution of $300,000 in cash. When it was discovered that we were not going to be able to raise that amount he had agreed to our selling 400 acres of land, but now the appraisal called for 520 acres.

"I remember when land in nearby Orange County was selling for a few dollars an acre and some of it is now selling for as much as $50,000 an acre," he said. "Almost any land in this part of the country sells for $5,000 an acre. You would be foolish to sell at this price. Whatever you do, don't sell it. And if you do, I withdraw my pledge of $300,000." I realized that Mr. Atkinson, because of his warm friendship and interest in the ministry, was seeking to prevent us from making an unwise move. Nevertheless, this was a crushing blow and as I took him down from my second-story office to his car, I could hardly wait to get back to my office before my emotions took charge. Back in my office, I closed the door behind me, fell on my knees and wept.

The miracle had become a mirage. All of our hopes and dreams had suddenly crumbled. In the attempt to meet the challenge of Mr. Atkinson's pledge, all of our fund-raising efforts were designed to raise the money for this project. Now since we had failed to meet this goal we were in an impossible position financially.

Not only could we not write off the debt, but we would actually lose the property unless God intervened immediately, and this possibility seemed rather remote in those bleak moments of discouragement. Furthermore, I would have to write the thousands of friends who had just read only a few days before that God had worked a miracle, and tell them that there had been no miracle at all. There was personal humiliation involved, of course. But worse than that, the cause of Christ would suffer, and many Christians would be confused.

What was I to do? I got out my Bible and looked for help and assurance. We are admonished and assured that "all things work together for good to them that love God, to them who are the called according to His purpose." [1] I read, ". . . without faith it is impossible to please him." [2] and ". . . The just shall live by faith." [3] I read a command from God which I had discovered some years before and which on various previous occasions had proved very meaningful to me. I was reminded that this is a command of God: "In every thing give thanks: for this is the will of God in Christ Jesus concerning you." [4]

Since the just are to live by faith and since "all things work together for good to those who love God," I do not know of a better way to demonstrate faith than to say "Thank You." So I got back down on my knees and thanked God for what had happened. I thanked Him through my tears. I thanked Him that in His wisdom and love, He knew better than I what should be done and that out of this chaos and uncertainty I knew would come a far greater miracle. There on my knees while I was giving thanks for this great disappointment, God began to give me the genuine assurance that this greater miracle was really going to happen.

Even so, the next day I began drafting the letter that would inform our friends that "our miracle" had been only a mirage. For some reason, however, I felt strongly impressed not to mail the letter.

A week passed. Ten days. Then Mr. Atkinson called and said that he would like to see me again. He said he had been talking to Arlis Priest and had an idea he thought might solve our problem. As soon as he arrived at Arrowhead Springs, he came directly to my office. "I would like to suggest that Campus Crusade for Christ borrow the money as an organization from the same insurance company that had offered to loan the money to the original twenty men; that we then invite the men who had originally agreed to purchase the land to sign the notes as guarantors," he said. "If you like this idea, I will still give Campus Crusade the $300,000 originally pledged." I was overjoyed at his offer. This meant that we would not have to sell our prized land, which we would one day no doubt need because of our rapidly expanding training program. The twenty men agreed to this new arrangement, for they had no interest at all in promoting their own financial gain, and they signed the note. Jess Odom, the president of the insurance company, a wonderful Christian and good friend of Campus Crusade for Christ, approved the loan at the lowest possible interest rate allowable.

The second miracle proved to be greater than the first. We still saved a large portion of the interest. Mr. Swig generously discounted his note $75,000 instead of $100,000 as he had originally offered, because of the lapse of time which now had taken place. So I tore up the letter of apology and in its place sent another explaining all that God had done.

Since my last letter sharing the miracle of Arrowhead Springs, God has done something even greater. The transaction about which I wrote has now been completed, resulting in a gift of $300,000 for Campus Crusade for Christ. There has been one change in the mechanics of the deal.

As I explained in my earlier letter, a part of the original plan involved the sale of a certain portion of the Arrowhead Springs property to a group of businessmen, friends who formed a corporation to make the purchase. The friend who had originally agreed to give his $300,000 pledge on the condition that the balance due on the mortgage be raised in the form of gifts, later agreed to fulfill his pledge even though raising the balance, on our part, involved the sale of 400 acres of the Arrowhead Springs property.

Plans for sale of the land were in the process of closing when the appraiser unexpectedly announced that 520 acres of land would be required to satisfy a one million dollar loan to the corporation. Realizing the present and potential value of the 520 acres in question, our friend generously offered to fulfill his pledge with the provision that Campus Crusade for Christ obtain the loan instead of selling the land.

This was a most generous and gracious act—a great concession over his original pledge. Also, our business friends who had organized a corporation to purchase the land generously agreed to sign the note as guarantors. If we should choose to sell the land later, the corporation is still willing to purchase.

To God be the glory, great things He has done! I wanted to take this opportunity to explain this change in plans so that our friends who have been so faithful to pray for and invest in this project would be acquainted with God's miraculous provision. Again, my sincere thanks to all who have been used of God to help make this miracle possible. Join with us in giving thanks and praise to Him.

Pray, too, for God's special blessing on the thousands who come to Arrowhead Springs for training in evangelism.

I shall be forever grateful to the Lord for Mr. and Mrs. Atkinson and for their encouragement in so many ways. After Mr. Atkinson went to be with the Lord memorial gifts from his family and friends were used to build a beautiful prayer chapel at Arrowhead Springs which has been dedicated to his memory.

Prior to and following the purchase of Arrowhead Springs, it has been our prayer that everything God would do through Campus Crusade for Christ and through our own personal lives would be characterized by the supernatural and the miraculous. We have asked Him to do things in such an unusual and wonderful way that men would *have* to say that He was responsible, and that they would give the glory to Him instead of to man. God has answered that prayer on many occasions. Since our arrival at Arrowhead Springs we have prayed that there might be such a worshipful atmosphere here that when people walk about the campus they will sense the presence of God. More than a few have indicated that their lives have been changed while visiting the campus, without anyone talking to them personally.

A few months after our arrival we faced a particular crisis that demanded a miracle. I received a call early one morning from Arlis Priest, stating that our large water reservoir was exhausted, that the water had disappeared mysteriously overnight, and that now, with a large staff and student group of 450 gathered for several weeks of training, there was absolutely no water for them. When we purchased the property we had been assured that there was plenty of water, but now we discovered that there was not enough water, at least not for us. This was one of the greatest of all the crises that had arisen for us at Arrowhead Springs.

The students and staff had paid thousands of dollars to come from far distances to be present for the training, and now our only alternative would be to send them home unless God worked a miracle to supply water. To return the students' money would be financially disastrous, for we would have to reimburse them, and all the money they had paid to us had already been used (we were operating on less than a shoestring). We had actually anticipated the revenue of the summer in making preparations for their coming. The maintenance and repairs for the facilities and the purchase of food took all the money; there was just no money left with which to reimburse them. Once again we were faced with the kind of crisis that could have meant the loss of this property and quite possibly the destruction of this ministry.

My first impulse was to panic; then, remembering again the admonition to give thanks in all things as an expression of faith, I fell on my knees, saying, "Lord, thank You for this crisis. I thank You that You will again demonstrate Your power and wisdom in our behalf." While on my knees I felt impressed to call George Rowan, who in drilling for steam had discovered large quantities of hot water on the property, and ask him if he had any idea of how we could convert the hot water well into drinking water. We had not used any of the hot water from the big well because we had been told that a cooling tower would cost at least $20,000; and since we didn't have even twenty dollars extra, this expense was far beyond our capabilities.

George informed me that he did not know how to cool the water but that he would check immediately with a friend of his, the president of a large geothermal corporation, who very likely could give us the information we needed.

Within a matter of a few minutes, his friend called me and told me over the telephone how a simple, inexpensive wooden cooling tower could be built. With the most rudimentary blueprint in hand, I rushed to the maintenance department and explained how the cooling tower could be built. Immediately, several staff members and a host of other volunteers, professionals and amateurs alike, began to work. By two o'clock the next morning cool water was running through the tower. Again, an impossible feat, but God heard our prayers.

One of the most beautiful parts of the whole experience, however, was the attitude of the staff and students about the crisis. They gathered in meetings, large and small, to thank God as an expression of their faith for this crisis in obedience to the command of I Thessalonians 5:18.[4] During the next twenty-four hours, a most remarkable spirit of cooperation and of cheerfulness pervaded the entire campus. Individuals were going to San Bernardino to buy small jugs of water and supplying their own needs and the needs of others. It was a beautiful experience of what happens to men who trust God and of how God honors faith. What better way to demonstrate faith than to say *Thank you*.

But these have not been the only times of testing. They are still frequent and almost continuous, but faith is like a muscle (it grows with exercise) and the more we know of the trustworthiness and faithfulness of God, His grace, love, power, and wisdom, the more we can trust Him. I think of my own faith: how in the beginning years of the ministry I could believe Him for a few dollars and on occasion, a few hundred; more recently I had been asking God for thousands.

For example, early in the ministry I discovered one day that we had an urgent need for $485. It was a Saturday morning and I was alone in the office. I was on my knees and praying for this $485 when the mailman came knocking on the door with a registered letter. I reached the door just as he was leaving, and he said, "It's a good thing you were here, or I wouldn't have been able to leave this letter." I signed for it, went back into my office to pray, but decided I would open the letter first. Inside, I discovered a bank note for $500 sent by a friend from far off Zurich, Switzerland, whose entire family had become Christians through our ministry.

Then I remember the day some years later when Breta Bate, our office manager, called to say that we needed $10,000 at once. "Do you know where we can get it?" she asked.

No, I didn't because, as usual, we had no surplus or collateral on which to borrow. The only thing (and the best thing I knew to do) was simply to ask the Lord. I suggested that she come over and we would pray together. Jesus had said, ". . . That if two of you shall agree on earth as touching any thing that they shall ask, it shall be done for them of my Father which is in Heaven." [5] So we asked God to supply $10,000 to meet this urgent need. We reminded the Lord that this is His work, and that to the best of our ability, we were seeking to do His will. We claimed the promise, ". . . if we ask any thing according to his will, he heareth us." [6] We needed the money to continue to serve Him. After prayer, since it was about six o'clock in the evening we went down to the dining room for dinner. An hour later, as I was walking back across the lobby of the hotel the telephone rang. It was a friend, Wes Ney, from Louisville, Kentucky, calling to say that I had been on his heart for a couple of days and though he was a new Christian at that time and was not used to this kind of leading, he wondered if the Lord was trying to tell him something about a particular need that we had. I told him that we had just been in prayer for $10,000. "You don't know anybody who has a surplus $10,000 floating around, do you?" I laughed.

He responded that that was a sizeable amount of money but that he would see what he could do and call me back within an hour. An hour later, he called to say that he was sending the $10,000. "Call it a loan without interest," he said. "I would like to make a gift later, but am not sure I can swing it at this time as I am short on cash." A year later, he wrote that we should write it off because his business had profited greatly and he wanted us to have the money.

At another time, an additional $48,000 was desperately needed to meet one of our annual payments on the loan. This kind of money does not come easily. We had prayed much and worked hard to raise the money, but to no avail. Our deadline was only days away when a lawyer friend who knew of our need introduced me to a friend who agreed to loan the amount needed for sixty days. I was in the lawyer's office ready to sign the necessary papers when my office called to tell me that Dean Griffith had called from Chicago and wanted me to contact him right away. Within minutes I reached him at his Chicago office. "I have been praying about your need for $48,000," he said, "and my father and I would like to send you a check for that amount today." Needless to say, I was grateful. As a matter of fact I got down on my knees and thanked the Lord that He had answered our prayers, and then I went out to share with our friends the good news that the loan was no longer needed. I offered to pay for the costs and inconvenience involved, but my offer was refused.

The purchase of Arrowhead Springs was a giant leap of faith. This facility would accommodate several times as many as could be housed at our training grounds on beautiful Lake Minnetonka in Minnesota. However, we soon found that it was not big enough. The first summer of 1963 found the big hotel and most of the other facilities filled, and by the second and third summers we were overflowing during the summer peaks. By 1966 we knew we would have to expand our facilities. Projections indicated that we would one day be training many thousands each week during the summer months and there was no place to train them, as present facilities were already taxed to capacity.

What were we to do? I called together a group of outstanding businessmen, planners, and builders for counsel. Norman Entwistle, our very able architect, drew up elaborate plans. Walter Gastil, a member of the board of directors and an outstanding Los Angeles businessman, who has been a great encouragement to me and to this ministry, agreed to chair an emergency fund-raising campaign called Operation Explosion. We needed large sums of money to provide these new facilities, as well as to meet other emergency needs resulting from the rapid growth and expansion of the ministry. Warren Bradley, an outstanding Los Angeles building contractor and dedicated Christian, agreed to construct whatever facilities we chose to build without profit to himself or to his company. We were under the pressure of deadlines. If we did not start building at once, it would not be possible to complete construction in time for the summer invasion of thousands of students. So, it was decided by the committee and the board of directors, that for emergency needs we would build a simple, inexpensive board-and-batten frame construction with a tar paper roof. We soon discovered we were building in an area where fire insurance premiums would be extremely high, and upon the recommendation of Warren Bradley and his brother Elmer, it was decided we would be well advised to build with slump stone and a tile roof. Norman Entwistle designed a beautiful complex of four dormitories and a dining-auditorium area that would accommodate a minimum of 480 and a maximum of 640, depending upon the number of people assigned to each room.

Though no funds were available for the construction of these buildings, the urgency of their completion was upon us and, after much prayer, we felt impressed to proceed with the building in the assurance that God would supply the funds to pay for their construction. The bulldozers had cleared the site, the foundations were being poured, and some of the walls were beginning to rise when a newcomer (who has since become a very good personal friend and strong supporter of Campus Crusade for Christ) appeared on the scene. He and Arlis Priest visited the building site and as they surveyed the hustle and bustle of the busy scene with workmen rushing to and fro hastening the construction of these urgently needed buildings, my friend turned to Arlis and said, "Who is going to pay for these buildings?"

Arlis said, "God impressed me to share this need with you."

Our friend dropped his head as if in silent prayer and meditation and then said, "I think I would like to be responsible to provide the funds for the building of these four dormitories. I need to talk with four of my associates and see if they are in agreement."

A short time later he came excitedly into my office to share his idea. He explained that he had been down to look over the site of the new Arrowhead Springs Village development and that he had felt impressed of the Lord to encourage his associates to join with him in paying for the project. "How much money will it take?" he inquired. "Approximately $550,000," I responded. "I think we can swing it," he said, "if we can work out a plan which will enable us to pay a certain amount each month over a period of years." Soon he was on the telephone contacting his associates and before long they were in unanimous agreement that this would be a good investment for the Lord's money which He had so graciously and so generously given to them. They were being good stewards. Here they saw a chance to multiply their dollars a hundred fold so that the tens of thousands of men and women who would be trained in this beautiful new addition would join with them to help take the claims of Christ to the entire world.

Later, I said to my friend, "What you are doing is such a challenging and inspiring example of Christian stewardship that I would like to prepare a plaque so that other friends of Campus Crusade for Christ will see what God has done through you and your associates. How would you like the plaque to read?"

Whereupon he responded, "My associates and I want to give God all the glory for the gracious way He has met our needs. Therefore, we would like for the plaque to read: ARROWHEAD SPRINGS VILLAGE, DONATED BY FIVE BUSINESSMEN WHO WANT TO GIVE GOD ALL THE GLORY. Later, a beautiful dining-auditorium building was constructed at a cost of $286,236, which amount our anonymous friends have asked the Lord to enable them to underwrite as well. Already, thousands of students and laymen from as many as 50 countries are being trained each year in these beautiful new facilities to be disciples for the Lord Jesus Christ. This gift is a true example of Christian stewardship—an example to other Christians to "lay up . . . treasures in heaven, where neither moth nor rust doth corrupt, and where thieves do not break through nor steal." [7]

Thus did we acquire a facility capable of providing quarters for thousands of students. With the acquisition of Arrowhead Springs our training program made giant steps forward.

8

The Secret:
Proper Training

I believe that there are three basic reasons why God has blessed the Campus Crusade ministry in such a phenomenal way: (1) dedication to exalting Jesus Christ and His cause in every circumstance; (2) a strong emphasis on the ministry of the Holy Spirit in the life of the believer; and (3) special, detailed, comprehensive training for every staff member.

The training ministry of Campus Crusade for Christ, under the direction of Dr. Ted Martin, coordinates the planning and execution of the various training programs of this ministry. This training insures that the staff, students, laymen, military personnel, and all persons associated with the ministry receive adequate instruction in the various training programs in which they are involved. The instruction includes principles of Christian living, principles and methods of evangelism and follow-up, as well as Biblical and theological training.

I first met Dr. Martin and his charming wife, Gwen, at our conference training center in Mound, Minnesota. Dr. Martin had earned his doctorate in theology at Dallas Theological Seminary and had been teaching at Multnomah School of the Bible. They explained that they were planning to go to the mission field. "However," they said, "before we go we would like to spend two years on the staff of Campus Crusade in order to learn more about evangelism. Would you be willing," they asked, "for us to come on the staff for two years with the understanding that we would then be free to go to the mission field?"

I agreed to the arrangement. That was ten years ago, and Ted and Gwen are still with us, for they discovered that the college campus is truly a mission field. For the past eight years Ted has been dean of the Institute of Biblical Studies and, more recently, also director of the staff training.

A manual covering this staff training has been written in an effort to help the Campus Crusade for Christ staff members prepare to meet the various situations that will confront them through their ministries. The material represents years of experience, many long months of compiling questions and answers and thinking through the many problems related to the various phases of the ministry. After several years of testing, the suggestions offered in our Staff Training Manual are given with the assurance that they will work if properly tried, for every idea and suggestion has been taken from the personal experience of the Campus Crusade staff.

One of America's Christian leaders and the head of one of the largest Christian organizations in the country was visiting one of our staff training sessions at which I had asked him to speak. In the course of our conversation, I showed him our Staff Training Manual. As he studied the table of contents and leafed through the manual of approximately 500 pages, he became increasingly excited. "If we had a staff training manual like this, it would multiply the effectiveness of our ministry a hundredfold." This is exactly what we feel our staff training methods and materials have done for Campus Crusade for Christ.

It all began while Vonette was working on her master's degree at the University of Southern California in preparation for a teaching career. She took a course in curriculum writing, under the direction of Dr. C. C. Crawford, a distant cousin. Dr. Crawford had perfected a how-to system of gathering information in which individuals involved in a particular project pooled needed information. Through this procedure, under Vonette's direction, different members of the staff have pooled their information and their experiences so that over a period of years we have developed a very comprehensive manual that deals with every possible problem that one could encounter in introducing students, professors, laymen, international students and others to Christ. Not only does it show how to reach them for Christ, but also how to build them in the faith.

Inspiration without perspiration leads to frustration and stagnation. Through the years it has been my privilege to attend all types of religious conferences, congresses, institutes, and retreats. I have been inspired to the heavens by eloquent addresses and sermons. However, more often than not, I have soon forgotten what it was that inspired me. Statistics on memory retention prove that I am not the exception, but rather that I am quite typical. Authorities in this field of research tell us that we forget 95 percent of what we hear for the first time. Our retention is better on the second and third hearings. However, in the case of a typical lecture we must hear it six times before we really remember it.

Time and again I have heard testimony given at various Christian conferences in about these words: "A year ago at this same conference I dedicated my life to Christ and I vowed that I would live for Him whatever it cost. I went away aflame for Christ, determined to capture my campus for the Lord (or to win my community to Christ)." But a year later the same individual would be back at the next conference saying, "I fell flat on my face after the first week (or the second week, or the first month) and I could hardly wait to get back up here so that I could get my spiritual gas tank filled and go back out to serve the Lord."

Since this type of comment and this mental attitude are so prevalent among Christians, we determined that in Campus Crusade for Christ we would major in perspiration rather than inspiration, that is, in the training of men and the building of disciples for our Lord. A strong emphasis is placed on the basics, which are reviewed again and again without apology. Repetition is one of the major factors in learning. Recently I had occasion to explain to our staff why we repeated the same basic messages and materials again and again as a part of our training. At the close of the meetings one of our directors, a seminary graduate, and former Presbyterian pastor said, "I would like to share with you a good illustration to help support your emphasis on the necessity of repetition. Years ago I was a member of a good church where the pastor repeated the basic Christian doctrines several times each year, much to the benefit of us all. Recently after nine years away, I returned for a visit and was encouraged to know that the pastor is continuing to preach and teach these same basic truths which made such an impact on my life.

"Later, I was associated with a very scholarly minister who polished each message like a beautiful gem. He never spoke on the same subject twice. You will be interested to know that I could not tell you one thing I learned from this great eloquent preacher, but much of what I know about Christ and the Bible I learned from my first pastor who believed in and practiced repetition."

We have discovered that when we truly train people, they are inspired to a height of dedication that one cannot possibly experience through inspiration alone. It is my strong conviction that true inspiration is the result of a very strong training program. From the very inception of this ministry our major thrusts have been: first, aggressive evangelism; then, training men; then, building disciples and sending them forth for Christ. Even in a conference in which a number of non-Christians are present, if the majority of those present are Christians, almost all of our messages are designed to build the Christian in the faith and challenge him to become a disciple. We train carnal Christians to become spiritual Christians, teaching them the difference between walking in the flesh and walking in the Spirit, and showing them how to share their faith in Christ more effectively with others. The end result is that within a matter of a few hours after the carnal Christians have become spiritual Christians and have learned how to communicate their faith, they begin to share Christ with the nonbelievers at the conference or institute. Thus, more people come to Christ through the awakened Christians than we could ever hope to reach for Christ through directing all of our messages toward non-Christians. Of course, the Christians are also greatly benefited through their experience of introducing others to Christ.

With this basic commitment to training and building disciples, Campus Crusade for Christ has first of all placed a strong emphasis on training the staff. We began this during the second year, when Vonette and I met with our six staff members at Forest Home and planned our training program for the coming year. There we began the preparation of materials for evangelism and follow-up. The second and third years our training program was held in the Campus Crusade for Christ lodge at Forest Home. Then we graduated to the beautiful campus of Westmont College. As the staff continued to grow, however, we found it necessary to secure still larger facilities, and in 1956 our training was conducted near the UCLA campus. Ultimately, of course, the training has been given at Arrowhead Springs, and now additional conference sites across the country are being utilized.

Our commitment to the necessity of training has led to the establishment of several effective programs.

Institute of Biblical Studies: This is a three-summer course of study lasting four weeks each summer, geared to a revolutionary spirit of Christian discipleship and evangelism with the goal of fulfilling the Great Commission in this generation. The entire curriculum is centered on the Bible and has been developed to provide solid biblical training that will help to equip Christians for roles in spiritual leadership in a world of crisis.

Leadership Training Institute: Hundreds of week-long and weekend training sessions held around the world each year are designed to teach students how to experience revolutionary Christian life and how to communicate it effectively to others in the power of the Holy Spirit.

Action Group Leaders' Conference: These sessions are designed to build disciples for strong, mature leadership roles in campus situations.

Athletic Conferences: Athletes are trained to experience personally and to share with others, especially other athletes, the adventure of the Christian life.

Music Leadership Training Institutes: Students and adults learn to serve Christ effectively in the ministry of music.

International Student Conferences: Students from other lands are won to Christ and trained as disciples to return to help evangelize their own countries.

Lay Institutes for Evangelism: Laymen are encouraged to become more vital and fruitful in their lives and witness for our Savior in their local churches, families, businesses and professions.

Pastors Institutes for Evangelism: These conferences are designed to encourage and assist pastors to be more effective and fruitful in their own personal lives and witness and more effective in their pulpits.

Through the years we have developed an entire series of "how-to's" or "transferable concepts," which have helped to make this a

76

revolutionary ministry. These concepts contain the distilled essence of the Christian life. For example, our experience has proved that we can teach these "transferable concepts" in a very short period of time to any sincere Christian who wishes to know them.

A "transferable concept" is a truth that can be communicated to another, who in turn will communicate the same truth to another, generation after generation, without distorting or diluting the original truth. This is what the Apostle Paul was saying to Timothy, his spiritual son in the faith, "For you must teach others the things which you and many witnesses have heard me speak about. Teach these great truths to trustworthy men who will, in turn, pass them on to others." [1]

A "transferable technique" is the vehicle, such as a tape, film or booklet, which is used to communicate a "transferable concept." For example, the Four Spiritual Laws booklet is a "transferable technique." The message contained in the Four Spiritual Laws booklet is a "transferable concept."

When Jesus gave the disciples the command to "Go ye therefore and make disciples of all nations, baptizing them . . . teaching them to observe all things . . . I have commanded you," [2] he was referring to certain truths which would enable His disciples to be more vital in their lives and more fruitful in their witness for Him.

Since like begets like and we produce after our kind, we cannot disciple others unless we are first discipled ourselves. I do not know how one can build a disciple without including all of the following "transferable concepts":

1. How to experience God's love and forgiveness.
2. How to be filled with the Holy Spirit.
3. How to walk in the control and power of the Holy Spirit.
4. How to witness for Christ effectively in the power of the Holy Spirit.
5. How to love by faith.
6. How to pray.
7. How to study the Bible.
8. How to grow in faith.
9. How to worship God.
10. How to know God's will for your life.

11. How to prepare a personal strategy to help fulfill the Great Commission in this generation.
12. How to train Christians to train others to learn the other transferable concepts.

It is true that no one can ever master these transferable concepts. I feel like a beginner myself after all of these years. Yet, it requires only a few weeks or months for any one who desires to be used of God to learn these "transferable concepts" and techniques well enough that they begin to be a part of his own life and he is able to pass them on to others. It is our objective to help train five million Christians to experience and share the abundant life in Christ by 1976 so that they in turn can help fulfill the Great Commission by 1980. These "transferable concepts" will help to accomplish this objective. We have a plan and we have the people to form the base for a growing pyramid. Utilizing our various special ministries, I believe we can and will, in the power of the Holy Spirit, accomplish the goal I have outlined. Now I should like to spell out more fully how some of our various programs operate and give some graphic examples that demonstrate their effectiveness. In one of them many readers may find an area of service that fits their own talents. We need all the help we can get.

9

The Key: The Campus

Upon my arrival at a large midwestern university it was announced that I was to have dinner and speak in the leading fraternity on campus. There was no time to check into the hotel, nor to get ready for the meeting. I was already late and consequently I rushed to the fraternity house. As I entered the living room, the fellows scattered as though I had leprosy. I wondered what was wrong and was puzzled by the coldness and the indifference of the men who remained in the room. Apparently someone had invited me without knowing who I was or anything about the nature of my message. No doubt they had decided in a subsequent fraternity bull session that they had no interest in a religious speaker, and my invitation to speak had been a mistake.

The president of the fraternity hardly spoke to me during the dinner hour. Obviously, he did not want any of his brothers to think that he was interested in religion. Finally, it became his painful duty to announce that there would be a "religious" meeting upstairs in the living room following the dinner hour. Without introducing me, he simply mentioned (in a tone that indicated he was not interested and anybody who was, was foolish) that a speaker from California would be speaking to those who were interested in religion.

I knew, as I observed the attitude of the men, that there would be no one present to hear me unless I acted fast. So I asked the president for permission to say a few words. Reluctantly, he granted me a few moments and I said to the men, "I have observed from your reaction that you are no more interested in religion than I am, and I want to put your minds at ease at once. I am not a religious speaker, nor am I here to talk to you about religion. As a matter of fact, I am opposed to religion. History records that religion has done more than any other one thing to keep man in ignorance and fear and superstition through the centuries."

This group of cold, indifferent, even antagonistic men had suddenly come alive. Some of them were dumbfounded, for they had been told that I was a religious speaker, and here I was, saying what was completely contrary to what they had anticipated. These and a few other well-chosen words had captured their attention.

By this time the men were ready to listen to anything I had to say, so I indicated to them that if they wanted to hear more I would meet with them upstairs in the living room.

Some of the men began to quiz me. "We thought you were a religious speaker," they said. "You don't sound very religious. What are you going to say?" Others, I discovered later, rushed to the telephone and called their friends in other fraternity houses and dormitories. They invited them to come and hear me speak, saying, "We have a religious speaker at our house tonight who doesn't seem to be very religious. We think you would enjoy hearing what he has to say. Come on over." By the time we gathered upstairs for the meeting the room was packed. Many additional men had come, out of curiosity to learn what I had to say.

"As I mentioned earlier," I began, "I am opposed to religion. But let me explain what I mean. By way of definition, religion is man's best effort to find God through his own good works whereas Christianity can be defined as God's search for man and the revelation of Himself in Christ. Because of man's many efforts to find God through the centuries, he has even resorted to criminal means, such as the Inquisition and the Crusades. The superstition of reincarnation and the belief that certain animals are sacred beings have caused masses to starve while animals survived. But I am not here to talk to you about how man can know God through his own efforts, because this is impossible for him to achieve. Rather, I am here to tell you how God became a man and visited this planet in the Person of Jesus of Nazareth. I am not here to talk to you about religion, but about a personal relationship with God made possible through the most remarkable Person who ever lived

—the God-man who changed the course of history: B.C., before Christ; A.D. *anno Domini,* in the year of the Lord."

For the next forty-five minutes I talked about Jesus—who He is; why He came to this earth; what He taught; the miracles He performed; His death on the cross for our sins; His resurrection; His message to men through the centuries; and His relevance to the collegian of today. When I finished no one seemed to want to leave. As usual, many expressed their desire to receive Christ.

Multitudes of students in fraternity, sorority and dormitory meetings on campuses across the country respond similarly when staff members of Campus Crusade for Christ present the Person of Christ—not religion, not Christianity in the broad general sense, not even the church, but a living dynamic Person. For those who say that religion and the church have no relevance for the student of today, we have good news. Each week several thousand staff, students and faculty are sharing the good news of Christ with thousands of other students and faculty who do not know who He is or how they can know Him. Jesus Christ is relevant. He is more relevant than anyone who has ever walked the face of this earth, and students by the tens of thousands are responding to His call, "Follow me."

You may be asking, "How do you account for this remarkable response to the gospel on the part of students when most people have been led to believe that students are not interested in Christ?" In addition to the spiritual emphasis, part of the answer is planning and strategy. Since the inception of this ministry our slogan has been, "Win the campus to Christ today, win the world to Christ tomorrow." Our strategy for accomplishing this is to expose men to the gospel, win them to Christ, build them in the faith, and send them forth to proclaim with us throughout the world the good news of the gospel.

Picture with your mind's eye a strategy room, a room with maps and charts and diagrams that tell the story of the college scene. Gathered around a rectangular table in this briefing room, twelve men are meeting with me for prayer and planning, seeking the mind and will of God as to how we can best evangelize the seven million students on three thousand campuses, who will assume leadership in tomorrow's world. These twelve men work with other men who, in turn, work with hundreds of others through a chain of command that enables us to recruit and train hundreds of additional staff each year and absorb them into a fruitful and effective ministry for Christ.

Seated at the head of the table with me is Rodney (Swede) Anderson, national coordinator of the campus ministry. Swede is a remarkably able and gifted young man with the finest credentials. He was an outstanding student at the University of Colorado, where he became a Christian through the ministry of Campus Crusade. Among other honors, he served as student body president of that university. Swede soon experienced the reality of walking in the Spirit by faith and became fruitful for Christ as a student. He married his campus sweetheart, Judy Kraus, who was the secretary of the student body. Swede enrolled at Dallas Theological Seminary where he continued to study for four years. Again, because of his many and remarkable qualities of leadership, he was elected to the office of student body president. In the meantime he continued to be the director of the Campus Crusade for Christ ministry in the Dallas area. Upon graduation Swede was assigned to direct the ministry in Philadelphia. After serving on the campus staff for seven years, he came to Arrowhead Springs to serve for one year as my personal assistant. He has now been assigned to coordinate the entire campus ministry.

At Swede's right is Jim Craddock. Jim has been a member of the staff for twelve years. He became interested in Campus Crusade while he was a youth pastor and a student at the University of Colorado, where he majored in public administration and minored in business and economics. As a youth pastor he had joined with others in praying that God would do something special on that campus. Soon after, Campus Crusade for Christ was invited to start a ministry there, and Jim became active as a member of the local advisory board. God called him to become part of the ministry of the staff upon his graduation from college. Through the years, Jim has continued to be one of the leaders whose influence is far-reaching and through whom thousands of men and women have been introduced to Christ directly and indirectly. Jim, with his wife, Doris, is now the south central regional director of the campus ministry.

Next to Jim, is Jim Green, who was a student at Wheaton College when I first met him. I remember the day he came to learn how to be filled with the Spirit. Jim had been a Christian most of his life. He had been reared in a godly home (his father is a professor at Wheaton College), and had heard the finest lecturers who had come to Wheaton with the most spiritual kind of messages, but he was not finding the Christian life easy to live, and he wanted to know what was wrong. We were in the process of starting a leadership training class at Wheaton College and a part of the instruction dealt with how to be filled with the Spirit. I made Jim promise that he would do everything our leader asked him to do and he diligently followed instructions. Later, he said, "As I came to understand the ministry of the Holy Spirit, especially how to be filled by faith, my whole life began to change. I became very interested in Campus Crusade. I used to go to one of the local secular colleges to witness regularly as a part of the Crusade training."

Jim was a biology major and a physical education minor and planned either to teach school or coach. While he was in the process of making his decision we had the opportunity to chat during one of my visits to Wheaton, and we discussed how every Christian can know the will of God according to the Sound Mind Principle of II Timothy 1:7: "For God has not given us the spirit of fear; but of power, and of love, and of a sound mind." I explained that since God has given us this sound mind we can use this God-given faculty to prayerfully evaluate what it is that God most wants to see accomplished in the world today and how our particular experience, training and abilities can make the greatest contribution toward accomplishing that goal.

I explained this to Jim in about five minutes and rushed away for another appointment. When I returned an hour later, Jim was so excited he was practically hanging from the rafters. He shared how God had not only told him what to do with his life but had indicated the movement with which he was to be associated. Now some six years later Jim Green, with his wife, Nan, is the regional director for the Big Ten area and, together with his staff, is making a mighty impact for God in helping to change the world.

Sitting by Jim is Bill Hogan. Bill had five years of training in two outstanding seminaries. Following seminary graduation he served for five years as assistant pastor in two very prominent Presbyterian churches. Then in his words, "I came to the point where I realized there was something missing in my ministry. I felt that above everything else the Lord wanted to use me and every Christian to bring others to Himself. Yet I knew of very few who had trusted Christ through my ministry. While attending a pastors' conference at Arrowhead Springs, I learned to use a few simple tools which have revolutionized my life in the area of evangelism. While there I was impressed not only with the value of the training but with the successful and strategic ministry of Campus Crusade. Desiring to sharpen my abilities as a witness and to use them in the most productive way possible, I felt impressed to apply for staff. These past five years have been more fruitful than I ever imagined they could be. My association with Campus Crusade has been a fulfilling experience." Because of his theological training and spiritual maturity, Bill exercises a wholesome and encouraging influence on staff, students, and laymen alike. With his wife, Jane, Bill directs the northeastern region where 104 of the first 119 colleges and universities were established as Christian schools. Harvard, Princeton, Dartmouth, Yale, William and Mary, and many others were all established, as expressed in the charter of Harvard University, "For the expressed purpose of perpetuating the Christian faith." It is a national tragedy that most of these schools no longer hold to their Christian heritage. In many cases, they are often even antagonistic to the Christian faith, rejecting as no longer valid the basic tenets which gave them birth, and prompting many educators and leaders to say that the greatest enemy of freedom and of the American way of life today is the university campus.

It is here that Bill and a great host of other dedicated staff members are taking the claims of Christ to tens of thousands of students regularly in an effort to win, build, and send men for the kingdom.

Jon Buell, with his wife Sandy, is the director for the southeastern region of the campus ministry. He first became acquainted with Campus Crusade while an art major at the University of Miami. Because of his remarkable ability, personality, and vast potential for Christ he soon began to demonstrate leadership for Christ as a student. Among other things, Jon was a student of communism and the more he saw of the success of this world conspiracy, the more alarmed and afraid he became. In the process, he became aware that the only hope for our world was Jesus

Christ, and he surrendered his life to Christ, not only as a means of his own salvation but to help bring to the rest of the world the message of Christ as the only answer to the threat of atheistic communism.

When I first met Karl Dennison he was student body president at Arizona State University, and was a concert pianist with a great future before him on the concert stage. However, he felt there was something lacking in his life. As he expresses it, "Through the program of Campus Crusade for Christ I became aware of a need in my life to establish a personal relationship with Christ. I received Him into my life, and later had the joy of introducing Arlene, my wife, to Christ. After graduation I toured Europe and Central America and became impressed that the key to reaching the world for Christ is through college students." It was while Karl was pondering the importance of the college world that Elmer Lappen, director of the Arizona ministry, invited him to speak to a student conference on the topic of "Christian Student Leadership." While he was speaking to these students God confirmed in his heart that he should invest his life in helping to change the world as a part of the Campus Crusade for Christ ministry. Karl is the northwest regional director of the campus ministry.

I cannot tell the story of Karl Dennison without parenthetically making reference to one of the most remarkable couples that I have ever known, Elmer and Lee Etta Lappen. The remarkable thing about Elmer and Lee Etta is the fact that for many years Elmer has been a victim of painful and crippling arthritis. In recent years he has spent most of his time in a wheelchair or in bed. Yet, under the strong leadership of this outstanding couple literally hundreds of students are reached for Christ year after year, and scores of these are finding their way into various Christian vocations. Each year for the last several years, a number of graduates from Arizona State University have become a part of the Campus Crusade for Christ official staff. Karl Dennison and a number of other student body presidents have become Christians and vital witnesses for our Savior through the influence of the great ministry of the Lappens. Elmer Lappen is not a spellbinder, an extrovert, nor an individual with unusual charismatic appeal. He is a humble servant filled with the Spirit, determined to make his life count for God. Few individuals on our staff have made a more significant and vital contribution than this dear man in the wheelchair and his devoted, loving and strong helper, Lee Etta. "Not by might, nor by power, but by my Spirit, saith the Lord of hosts," [1] is demonstrated in the life of this couple in remarkable measure.

Jimmy Williams is next, as my eye travels around the table. One of our staff members had introduced to Christ an outstanding football player, who had lived a godless and immoral life at the University of Texas. The change this brought about in his life was so dramatic that Jimmy Williams, a student at SMU, was greatly impressed. Jimmy had a beautiful singing voice, and during his college years he was a featured nightclub entertainer. Later, Carol Kinney, an attractive young coed at SMU, who later became his wife, demonstrated through her life and witness a reality of the same risen Christ. Soon Jimmy capitulated to the Savior. Following graduation, he enrolled at Dallas Theological Seminary for four years. While there he continued active as a part-time staff member of Campus Crusade for Christ. Upon graduation Jimmy became the full-time director of the ministry in that area. Later he became the regional director of the southwestern states of the campus division.

In addition to these regional directors, seven very dedicated and highly qualified young women also give themselves unstintingly as they travel from campus to campus building disciples among women staff and students. They are: Judy Mold, Becky Rieke, Jean Pietsch, Ney Bailey, Esther Boomstra, Ruth Ann Jackson, and Thera Smith. These dedicated young women are carrying on the tradition established by Shirley Mulligan Hinkson, Diane Ross Hutcheson and Mary Lou Starr, whose lives have had a mighty impact in the States and continue to have an impact in Europe and Asia.

Also seated at the table is Frank Obien, another outstanding student, who graduated with honors from UCLA. Upon graduation, he joined the Campus Crusade staff and, with his wife Rosemarie, served several years as a staff worker in the United States and two years in the Philippines. Frank's mother and father were Filipinos. Though they moved to the United States soon after Frank's birth, his ties with the Orient remain. As a staff member, Frank had been fruitful in his work with students, especially international students. Thus, when it became necessary to appoint a director for our international student ministry, Frank was the logical choice. Today he is responsible for giving leadership to the rest of the staff in seeking to reach for Christ all of the 115,000 students from various countries of the world who are attending schools in the United States. The mission field has come to us, and we must reach these students with the claims of Christ. Key laymen are invited to open their homes to international students for the purpose of witnessing to them of Christ. Others are invited to participate in the various campus programs in the areas in which they live and study. Frank's part of the strategy session is to make sure that the mission field that has come to us is not overlooked.

Next to him is Dr. James F. Engel. Dr. Engel is one of the most remarkable college professors in America. He is the coordinator of the Campus Crusade for Christ ministry to the professors of America and is a full professor at Ohio State University in the department of marketing. He is recognized as one of the leading authorities in that field in America, with five major books and many articles to his credit. With his wife, Sharon, he devotes all of his free time to giving leadership to the faculty ministry of the campus division.

Jim and Sharon Engel came into a vital, living relationship with Christ only within the past few years. So great has been the change in their lives, that they want to share their faith with anyone and everyone who will listen. When I learned of their zeal for our Savior I invited them to come to Arrowhead Springs for one of our faculty conferences. Together, we discussed the challenge of reaching the college and university faculty members of the United States. As coordinator of the faculty ministry, Dr. Engel visits scores of campuses where he meets with professors, challenging them to take a more vital and vigorous stand for the Savior and encouraging them to join with us in helping to reach the university world for Christ.

At Ohio State Dr. Engel took the initiative in calling together several faculty members who began to meet and study together for one purpose, to reach their colleagues and students for Christ. As more faculty became involved, the group held its first campus-wide effort at an annual prayer breakfast for faculty administration. The response was so encouraging that the prayer breakfast has continued to be an annual affair with as many as 300 in attendance.

When Dr. Engel was asked if this has made a difference on the campus, his reply was, "Yes, definitely, many lives have been changed, some have met Christ for the first time. Others have found rededication and a new focus for their faith. Key men and women of all walks of campus life are now beginning to claim more openly that they are Christians. This is not easy because we have to face opposition from a variety of sources. Yet the louder the voices of protest, the more dynamic the movement seems to become. Campus Crusade for Christ has played a major role in the faculty story of Ohio State University. And under its impetus vital Christian activity among the faculty is spreading around the country. The faculty ministry of Campus Crusade for Christ was formed in the spring of 1967 and hundreds have been trained already at conferences at Arrowhead Springs and elsewhere to share their faith more effectively, using modern tools and procedures. We are praying that tens of thousands of professors will become involved in helping to bring Christ back to His rightful place of authority in the classrooms of America.

Dave Hannah, director of the athletic ministry of the campus division, was one of the outstanding football players in America when he was introduced to Christ by Swede Anderson. As a new Christian his zeal for the Savior knew no bounds, and his vision for helping to evangelize the world soon led to his helping to expand this ministry to athletes. From the inception of this ministry, athletes have always played a major role in this work. For some reason, perhaps because of the discipline of the sports or because of the high standards set by most coaches and leaders in the area of athletics, athletes have usually been responsive to the gospel. When they become Christians they often excel in effectiveness because they carry over into the Christian life the same disciplines that have helped them to be outstanding athletes. Dave Hannah is one of these. Under his leadership the Athletes in Action basketball team, the wrestling team, and the weightlifting team have been used of God to reach tens of thousands for Christ.

These men seated around the table are representative of a campus ministry that is dedicated to blanketing the three thousand campuses of the nation with the gospel and to confronting each of the seven million students with the claims of Christ.

To achieve this goal, planning is very important. In the providence of God two remarkable young men are participating in this meeting to help give leadership in this strategic area of planning. In the summer of 1968, four young men visited my office at Arrowhead Springs. They were about to begin their second year of graduate study in the master's program at the Harvard Graduate School of Business Administration. Two of them had been active in Campus Crusade for Christ as undergraduates, and all four had become active in our work in Boston in their first year of graduate study at Harvard. They were interested in making their lives count for Christ, but they were not sure how to do so. They felt God might be calling them to Campus Crusade.

Needless to say, I was very interested. Two of our greatest needs are planning and men trained in the area of business. As we interacted together it became apparent that God wanted these men to be more active in the ministry during their second year. As a result, under the supervision of one of their professors they undertook a special study—a report on the entire international ministry of Campus Crusade for Christ. This project earned them the highest grade their professor had ever given on such a project. When they came to make their report at the end of their school term they did so with great anticipation. I greeted them with equal enthusiasm. Their recommendations were exciting and proved to be an expansion of plans that many of our leaders in various divisions of the Crusade ministry and I had discussed previously. Here were men with fresh, new insights on how to implement and expand this worldwide ministry. These four young men, Bruce Cook, Steve Douglass, Larry Edge, and Jim Heiskell, had interviewed more than a hundred of our staff across the nation, had spent considerable time with the heads of the various divisions and departments, and now they had come to make their report to me personally.

They had flown all the way from Harvard to meet with me at Arrowhead Springs. They had come with their charts and diagrams and proposals. It was apparent, as they unfolded their findings, that they were watching my every reaction and after two hours of their presentation—in which each of the four participated—they asked me what I thought. I was elated. As a matter of fact, I was so excited that I observed some of the report through misty eyes. Here were men whom God had raised up to help us achieve our goal of a worldwide ministry. And when they had finished their presentation, I asked, "Who is going to help implement these plans?" Whereupon two of the men, Bruce Cook and Steve Douglass, said, "We are prepared to come full time." Larry Edge and Jim Heiskell said, "Because of previous commitments, we would like to become a part of the associate staff and give as much of our free time as possible to assisting in the local ministries where we work." This was an ideal arrangement for us, and immediately the men went to work.

All of these men had been outstanding: Jim at Vanderbilt, Larry at Yale, Bruce at Georgia Tech, and Steve at MIT. They had all received outstanding honors both in graduate and undergraduate school. Steve graduated from Harvard Graduate School of Business Administration with high distinction (upper 2 percent of the class). Here were men who could be making large salaries (as could other members of our staff) from $15,000 to $25,000 a year. Now they were coming to serve Christ on the same basis as the rest of the staff, as missionaries responsible for raising their own support. There is quite a difference between $285 a month which they have to raise themselves and the $15,000 to $25,000 a year which they had been offered or could expect to receive.

As campus coordinator, Swede was leading our discussion. We were considering by what means we could hope to fulfill our objective of saturating all the college and university campuses of the United States with the gospel by 1976, and recruiting tens of thousands of disciples to help fulfill the Great Commission in this generation. Eighteen years of experience had enabled us to develop a basic philosophy and a strategy that was already having phenomenal impact. Now we were meeting to consider how we could more effectively implement this program and accelerate both the recruiting of staff and the communicating of the claims of Christ to additional millions of students. The discussion centered around the fraternity, sorority and dormitory meetings, personal appointments, classroom meetings, College Life, leadership training classes, action groups, and special events such as using free speech platforms. Such topics may have little meaning to some, but to the men gathered around this table they represent effective means that are being employed to challenge tens of thousands of students week after week with the claims of Christ and the demands of Christian discipleship.

90

10

A Strategy for Colleges

A typical fraternity, sorority, or dormitory meeting usually involves a team of three or four men, if speaking to men, or a mixed group if speaking to women. One of the group emcees and shares his personal commitment to Christ. He then introduces other members of the team who give brief two- or three-minute presentations of what Jesus Christ means to them and how He has changed their lives. Finally a member of the staff, or a more mature, trained student leader, brings a brief presentation of the claims of Christ: who He is, why He came to this earth, and how the student can know Him personally in a life-changing experience. At the conclusion of the presentation opportunity is given to those who wish to commit their lives to Christ to bow in a prayer of commitment with the speaker.

It has been our experience that an average of 25 to 50 percent of the non-Christian students in the original meetings are interested in making this commitment. Though not all of the ones who offer this prayer give evidence of new life at that time, many thousands do. On the basis of almost twenty years of experience, there is reason to believe that many who do not demonstrate spiritual birth and growth in the beginning, later reaffirm their commitment and do become vital Christians. Of course there are some from whom we never hear again.

Many adults automatically assume that college students are not interested in religion and in the church, and in this assumption they are correct. However, the average student is interested in the

Person of Jesus Christ, and for many years we have made this distinction in our presentation. We do not talk about religion or the church, though we believe in the church and require that every staff member become an active member of a local church within ninety days after arriving at his permanent assignment. We also encourage all the students to become active church members. However, at our first encounter our message emphasizes the Person of Jesus. Students are sometimes antagonistic when we first arrive, assuming that we are going to give them the bit about religion and the church, which they have long since rejected.

I remember one such experience when I arrived with a team to speak in an outstanding fraternity house. We arrived in time for dinner, as per the invitation, and it was arranged that we would make our presentation following the dinner hour. While I was sitting beside the president during the meal he revealed to me that he was faced with a very serious problem. Though he was not a Christian, he was sympathetic with our cause and felt that he should warn me that several of his brothers were planning to embarrass us and cause us to leave the fraternity house in defeat and humiliation. The ringleader of this plot was one of the outstanding students on campus, a moral reprobate who had an unholy disgust and dislike for anything religious or Christian. He was determined to make us the laughingstock of the campus and had rallied several of his fraternity brothers to his cause over the objection of the president.

As the president and I conferred, I felt impressed to recommend to him that he exercise his authority as president and require that every member of the fraternity attend the meeting, and that he leave the rest to us. Though I did not tell him so, I was leaving the rest to the Lord. The brothers were somewhat disgruntled when the president announced that their attendance at the meeting was required.

Anticipating their disgruntlement and unhappy presence, we greeted them with a bit of humor and then proceeded to explain to them that we were not there to play games. We were there to talk about the most revolutionary Person the world has ever known, a Person who made revolutionary claims for Himself and revolutionary demands upon all who would follow Him. We made it clear that there were a lot of people who did not have the intestinal fortitude to be His followers, and asked all of those who felt that they had the potential to be His followers to put aside their preconceived ideas and listen to what was being said as though their lives depended upon it, as indeed their eternal lives did.

The whole atmosphere of the house changed. The men responded to the challenge, and when the opportunity was given for those who wished to receive Christ over half of the men, including the president and the leader of the original plot to embarrass us, marched with me into the fraternity den. There we had the opportunity to explain to them further how they could know Christ. We had prayer with them and made plans for the beginning of a weekly Bible study. Different members of the team made appointments with those who had responded, as well as with other members of the fraternity who had attended the original meeting. Throughout the remainder of the week these appointments were kept and further commitments to Christ were made.

Appointments for subsequent personal interviews are usually made by a member of the team approaching a member of a house and asking, "What did you think of that meeting?" The response is usually "Great! Wonderful! I've never heard anything like it." The next question is, "Did it make sense?" "It sure did," is the reply. "Would you like to get together and talk about it?" The answer is almost always in the affirmative. Often, when there is no rush to leave, a team member will pursue the matter further, if the individual responds that what he heard made sense. The team member will ask if he would like to talk about it at that point, and together they consider the Four Spiritual Laws, and then pray together. Thousands of students have been introduced to Christ following meetings of this kind. It is also an approach that many laymen use following church services or similar meetings which non-Christians are invited to attend.

A meeting of this kind is always bathed in prayer. The team members meet one hour before the time of departure for a time of special briefing on what each team member is to say and how he is to say it; to check each other on the way they are dressed; and then, finally, to pray for God to work in the hearts of the students. They are conscious of the fact that unless God speaks through their lips there can be no spiritual harvest, for Jesus said, "No man can come to me, except the Father which hath sent me draw him." [1]

93

By faith each team member acknowledges his dependence upon the Holy Spirit and appropriates the fullness of God's power; and the group is on its way, in joyful anticipation of what God will do.

Dr. Earl Radmacher, president of Western Baptist Theological Seminary in Portland, Oregon, was invited by Bud Hinkson, then our Oregon director, to participate in a meeting of this kind. He later reported that he had never before been in so many prayer sessions about a single meeting. He said, "We met together for prayer before we left, we prayed on the way to the meeting in the car, we prayed when we got to the assignment before we got out of the car, all of us continued in a spirit of prayer before the meeting, and on the way home we prayed, thanking the Lord for what He had done, asking Him to continue to work in the hearts of the students. Never before had I seen such a great volume of prayer surrounding any other Christian activity. I concluded that these people associated with Campus Crusade for Christ must be truly dependent upon the Lord, or they wouldn't pray so much."

Dr. Radmacher's observation pretty well sums up my attitude and that of the average Campus Crusade for Christ staff member or student worker. Working as we are with the intelligentsia, college students and professors, we know that it is not enough to depend upon logic, eloquence, brilliance or persuasiveness. We are engaged in a spiritual ministry, a ministry of changing men's lives, a supernatural ministry. Therefore, we must depend upon supernatural resources to accomplish supernatural objectives. That is the reason for our international 24-hour chain of prayer, in which men and women around the world are participating as they engage in believing prayer for a mighty moving of His Spirit.

In addition to thousands of teen meetings as I have just described, there are also hundreds of College Life meetings held each week on campuses across the nation; they are attended by scores and hundreds of students, as many as 1,000 on some campuses and on special occasions by several thousand. College Life meetings are usually held in the living room of the largest fraternities and sororities on the campus, or in a dormitory or student union building. The program includes lively singing, individual sharing of personal faith in Christ, and an appropriate message from a staff member, a local pastor or layman.

Following this meeting, which is usually one of the most exciting occasions of the week, trained members of the staff and students are on the alert for visitors and guests who may not know the Savior. The usual questions are: What did you think of the meeting? Did the message make sense? Have you made this wonderful discovery of knowing Christ personally? You would like to, wouldn't you? Thousands of students through the years have responded in the affirmative, and new life has begun.

You may wonder why so many students on a single campus attend such meetings week after week. First of all, the programs are designed to be attractive, warm, exciting, and again, bathed in prayer by the vital Christians on campus. Second, in addition to the usual reminders of weekly postcards mailed to the regular attendants and others they wish to invite, and the ads in the local student newspaper, groups of students in organized fashion go in automobiles to pick up those who need rides, if the meeting place is some distance from where the students live; or, the students may go in teams to speak with various groups at the dinner hour, reminding them of the College Life meeting to be held later in the evening. Others go from door to door in dormitories and other living quarters, knocking on doors and inviting people to attend personally. Scores of students are involved in committees that are responsible for various activities contributing to a successful meeting. These large meetings do not just happen, but, because of dedicated, Spirit-filled lives, a lot of hard work, and prayer, the students show up in large numbers. As a result, many come to know our Savior and join in helping to change their campus for Christ.

Campus Crusade for Christ is committed to aggressive evangelism. By aggressive evangelism I mean going to men with the good news of our living Christ and His love and forgiveness, not in argumentative tones nor with high pressure techniques, but taking the initiative to tell (as the Apostle Paul wrote) all men everywhere about Christ. We realize that this can best be accomplished by multiplication rather than through addition. This is the reason training is so important and has been since the inception of this ministry. Each week on hundreds of campuses the leadership training classes are held in which thousands of students learn how to experience and share the abundant life in Christ.

Thousands of students who have been living in spiritual defeat, who have never learned how to introduce others to Christ, are greatly benefited through the instruction they receive in the leadership training classes. Those who participate in the classes are encouraged to become involved in smaller action groups. It is the purpose of these action groups to put into practice the training received in the leadership training classes. As smaller groups of a half dozen or so encourage one another in their Christian walk and witness and share and pray and witness together, their lives are enriched for Christ and their relationship with one another is beautifully enhanced. Because of these small action groups and leadership training classes, there develops a great bond of Christian love and camaraderie reminiscent of first century Christians, whose love for one another has been extolled.

Thousands of students are being introduced to Christ through team meetings in fraternities, sororities, and dormitories; in personal appointments; through College Life meetings; and through special events, such as André Kole, our various athletic teams, and the New Folk and Forerunners singing groups. Nevertheless, the men who sit around the strategy table are asking one another and the Lord: "Are there not other ways to reach additional millions? Surely, somehow the message of Christ can be communicated to millions of students who are not now being confronted with the good news concerning Jesus Christ."

Out of this and other strategy sessions have come ideas to distribute literature to millions of students, to correspond personally with hundreds of thousands of students, to offer them—through ads in newspapers and student magazines—literature to help them know who Christ is and how they can grow in their Christian faith. As these plans are implemented, we anticipate that millions of students will commit their lives to Christ and tens of thousands will become His disciples. The men who are seated around this strategy table with their maps and charts and diagrams are revolutionists. They, together with our staff throughout the world, are spiritual revolutionists—men who have committed their lives in forty-three countries of the world, to the fulfillment of the Great Commission in our generation. These men realize that the college campus represents the greatest source of manpower immediately available to accomplish this objective. They agree with Billy Graham, that the struggle for the minds of men is going to be decided in the halls of learning throughout the world.

11

Berkeley — A New Kind of Revolution

Berkeley is a name that has become synonymous worldwide with student riots, demonstrations and radical movements of all kinds. Professors long associated with the university now believe that its radical influence has greatly hindered the effectiveness of the instruction at this school, which was once rated one of the greatest universities in the world.

As Christians and as members of the Campus Crusade for Christ staff, we were concerned that so little was being accomplished for Christ on this campus, the fountainhead of the radical movement. So, at one of our campus strategy sessions it was decided that we would call together 600 of our staff and students from across the nation and invade the University of California with the good news of Christ through a week-long convention. Our theme was "Solution—Spiritual Revolution."

A syndicated news release from Berkeley carried this story:

A new kind of revolution talk was heard today on the steps of Sproul Hall on the campus of the University of California at Berkeley. This site has been the scene of student protests and demonstrations and unrest for several years, but today about 3,000 students gathered to hear about a different kind of revolutionary leader—Jesus Christ. The occasion was a rally put on by the Berkeley chapter of the Campus Crusade for Christ, an organization which is having its national convention this week in the Berkeley student union building. While other students passed out handbills for and against the firing of the University of California president, Clark Kerr, and others distributed buttons reading, "Impeach Reagan," a folk singing group sang gospel songs with a contemporary sound and the Campus Crusade leader proclaimed a new kind of revolution. The students were asked to trust Christ as the One who has the answers to all the problems of the day and the One who can bring spiritual revolution and change to the world. They claimed that the Christian message is revolutionary because it has changed history, creating vast social reforms through reshaping the lives and attitudes of individuals. The Campus Crusade rally on the Sproul Hall steps came at a time of special turmoil and tension on the Berkeley campus because the day previously the Board of Regents had fired President Clark Kerr. As a result, newsmen and television cameras were on hand for the rally assuming that students were planning a major demonstration over the firing of Kerr. Instead, they were greeted by the Campus Crusade revolutionaries who had reserved this area some weeks prior to the firing of President Kerr. Inasmuch as they had the use of the air, it was impossible for the radicals to drown out the demonstration, and both of the major television networks commented on the fact that Berkeley was the quietest campus in all the University of California system because of the influence of the Campus Crusade for Christ on the Berkeley campus.

Had it not been for our presence there few doubt that the Berkeley campus would have been the scene of the most radical of all the demonstrations in the state. But day after day throughout the Sproul Hall area, different members of the staff and students presented musical programs and gave their witness for Christ. Among the most outstanding was the presentation by illusionist André Kole whose remarkable ministry is detailed elsewhere in this book.

One local newspaper described the "invasion" in this way:

Unparalleled Organization. Campus radicals, accustomed to being hailed the best student organizers, looked on in amazement as the extensive Campus Crusade for Christ campaign got under way in an attempt to evangelize the entire student body at Berkeley. Teams of delegates spoke and shared their faith in Christ in more than 70 dormitories, fraternities, sororities and nearby student residences. Other groups spoke and sang in restaurants, coffee houses and similar gathering places for "free speech movement" advocates, and other teams of delegates conducted a door-to-door campaign in the entire area adjacent to the campus just to make sure that no one was overlooked in the crusader's effort to give each of the 27,000 students an opportunity to hear the claims of Christ on their lives.

In addition to the regular convention schedule of morning and evening addresses, daily Bible exposition and prayer sessions, staff members also spoke in nearby churches and in church related meetings.

More than half of the students in most of the fraternities, sororities and dormitory meetings indicated that they would like to know how to become Christians. A young man from Hawaii, who was visiting at Berkeley, made his decision in a restaurant after a third Crusade delegate, during that one week, had talked to him about his personal relationship with Christ.

By the time the week-long convention had ended, over 700 had made similar commitments to Christ, and approximately 2,000 other students indicated that they would like to know more about Jesus Christ and how they also could commit their lives to Him. These are being followed up by members of the staff who remained after the convention with the regular staff to counsel the new converts and help the inquirers to make their commitment to Christ.

The week at Berkeley, beginning Sunday afternoon with an athletic banquet, was filled with exciting potential. All Cal athletes were invited, and some 400 of these responded to hear a number of famous athletes give their testimonies. I had the privilege of presenting additional good news of Christ to these men and of inviting them to receive Him as their Savior. A number of Berkeley's outstanding athletes responded to the invitation.

The following morning 125 student leaders, representing a good share of the student government leadership of the university campus, attended the student leadership breakfast where the students heard testimony from State Senator John Conlan of Arizona and

Larry Gonzales, Florida State University student body president, as they shared their faith in Christ. Again I followed with a salvation message explaining who Christ is, why He came and how they could know Him personally. A number of these leaders responded.

During the course of the week, twenty-eight dinners were held for international students. The gospel was presented at each of these and many of these students from a number of foreign countries were introduced to Christ. Scores of additional meetings were held on and off the campus. Meetings continued from noon until after midnight in the Forum on Telegraph Avenue, a hangout for the radical students, the street people and the hippies at Berkeley. Approximately forty of these radicals prayed to receive Christ during that week. Each evening approximately 1,400 students gathered in the Berkeley Community Theater to hear the Campus Crusade staff present the claims of Christ.

A unique feature of the week of campus saturation was the battery of twenty telephones that were installed in one of the fraternity houses leased for the occasion. Upon arriving at the university, each of the 600 delegates was given a list of names (thousands of students' names were divided among the 600 delegates) and from early morning until late at night the telephones were in use as calls were made requesting appointments to talk to the students personally about Jesus Christ. Thousands of students made appointments for interviews and hundreds of these made commitments to Christ.

Billy Graham arrived for the last day of the meetings. Upon his arrival at the airport a press conference was held in which reporters interviewed Billy and me. Early the next morning a special breakfast was held for approximately 300 of the faculty in the Student Union. Billy gave a powerful presentation of the gospel, and I had an opportunity to explain the purpose of our week at Berkeley.

Friday proved to be a dramatic day. Following the evangelistic faculty breakfast there was to be a great rally at the Greek Theater at noon with Dr. Graham. Dawn greeted us with a downpour of rain. The rain continued all morning, and as we met in our various sessions we prayed that God would stop the rain in time for the noon rally. As we continued to pray, the rain continued to pour. What were we to do? Surely God had not brought us to this great week of witness for Christ and finally to the grand climax meeting for us to fail. There was no other place to meet and the Greek Theater has no roof; thus, surely thousands who would otherwise come would be forced to miss hearing the gospel through Billy's message because of the rain.

Whatever we ask in prayer believing we shall receive . . . If we ask anything according to His will, He hears us, and if He hears us, He answers us. . . . God is not willing that any should perish but that all should come to repentance. These and many other promises of Scripture were claimed as we asked God to intervene and stop the rain. As we asked God, the Creator of heaven and earth, the One who controls men and nations and all of nature, to intervene for the salvation of souls, dramatically and abruptly it happened—the rain stopped. The clouds parted and the sun shone through. God had answered our prayers. A spontaneous song of praise flowed from our hearts as we realized the rally in the Greek theater would take place as planned.

We adjourned our meeting in the Student Union to make our way up the hill to the Greek Theater. A total of some 8,000 students and faculty joined us to hear Dr. Graham. Following his clear-cut presentation of the gospel, he invited the students on this great campus to commit their lives to the King of kings and the Lord of lords. Long after the meeting was over 600 staff and students were counseling and praying with those who had remained behind to learn how they could become Christians. God had done a mighty work at Cal but this was not the end, only the beginning.

After most of us left Berkeley, those remaining began a follow-up program designed to preserve and increase the impact that had been made. All of the students who had invited Christ into their lives, and those who expressed interest in knowing more, were contacted during the first week after the convention and approximately 200 of these who had just received Christ attended a retreat to learn more about how to live the abundant Christian life. Many hundreds who expressed interest in learning more about the Christian faith were contacted and given the opportunity to investigate further what Christ could do in their lives. Many of these responded as well. The 600 staff and students who had participated in the Berkeley convention will not soon forget Berkeley; according to one of the university's most distinguished professors, one who has served more than thirty years on the faculty, Berkeley will not soon forget Campus Crusade for Christ.

12

Reaching High-School Students

Shrieking whistles called the first Titusville High home football game to a standstill as highway patrolmen and sheriff's deputies flooded the field and stadium, helping the thirty-man Titusville, Florida, police force restore order in the face of racial dissension that had erupted into savage fights. Injured people were hospitalized and others were arrested, and the front pages of the nation's papers featured "racial unrest in Titusville."

On the following Monday near civil war broke out on campus with fights, injuries and reports of students carrying concealed weapons. Desperate for a solution, the principal asked Paul Williams, a student at Brevard County Junior College, to bring some outstanding Negro and white personalities to speak to the student body. Paul had been trained by Campus Crusade and had started a rapidly growing Christian group at the high school.

Working with the High-School Ministry of Campus Crusade for Christ (he later joined the high-school staff) Paul brought in speakers who presented the claims of Christ to the entire student body of 2,500, reaching to the very roots of the racial problem. About 100 students who attended the Christian meeting had been trained to present effectively the Four Spiritual Laws with classmates interested in knowing more about the Christian life. Some 100 students prayed to receive Christ that day; several of them were key militants on both sides of the racial strife. The atmosphere at Titusville High School was radically changed, as Christian students demonstrated the power of God's love through Jesus Christ.

The High-School Ministry of Campus Crusade is using two forms of ministry; organizing, training and leading youth in city-wide youth crusades, and working with local churches and communities in forming a youth program that is school-oriented and aimed at carrying on a continuous program of evangelism. Staff members and teen-agers share Christ with their friends and seek to establish them in the fellowship of the church for further follow-up.

In San Bernardino, California, Lauren Littauer decided to make her speech class a platform for Christ. For "a description of a place" she told about Arrowhead Springs and its Christian message. She used "Peanuts" and a Christian message for her talk on "Comedy," and convinced her teacher of the second coming of Christ in her third talk. She received grades of A−, A, and A+, and the thrill of seeing several of her classmates come to know Christ.

The use of drugs had become widespread in Troy High School in Orange County, California. God did a miracle in the life of one of the members of the Troy High School basketball team. This boy had been involved with drugs. After accepting Christ, he immediately began to share his faith with others. In one month, more than 120 students, including most of the basketball team and cheerleaders; accepted Christ.

In Florida the title of Maitland's Junior Miss went to a Winter Park High School senior who presented the Four Spiritual Laws in three languages as her talent in that section of the contest. Also voted Miss Congeniality, Donna Rapacz saw several other contestants discover a new life in Christ.

The high-school student of today is more knowledgeable concerning world affairs and the domestic problems than were the collegians of earlier generations. Furthermore, the average high-school student today, when won and discipled for Christ, often demonstrates unusual zeal and commitment. For example, the militant groups such as the Communists, Black Panthers, and others have said that they are particularly interested in reaching high-school students for their causes because they believe that this age group supplies the best and most lasting disciples.

The number of high-school students in America doubled during

104

the last ten years, from 7.8 million in 1958–59 to nearly 14.1 million in 1968–69. Today there are 12,250 high schools in the United States.

James E. Allen, Jr., U.S. Commissioner of Education, recently pointed out that the secondary schools represent the greatest area of threat and disturbance in the nation. During a four-month period in the last year more than 340 schools in thirty-eight states experienced serious student disturbances. The number of incidents is likely to increase this year. Crime statistics throughout America reveal that the use of drugs and alcohol is spreading like wildfire among high schools. It is estimated by juvenile authorities that 50 to 85 percent of the high-school students are either using or have experimented with some form of drugs. Arrests of persons under eighteen years of age are increasing faster than in any other age group—a 69 percent increase in seven years. Immorality is widely accepted. Venereal disease increased 232 percent in the 15- to 19-year age group in a seven-year period. Pregnancies have soared in number.

The High-School Ministry of Campus Crusade began in the fall of 1966, under the direction of Carl Wilson and his wife Sara Jo. Carl graduated at Fuller Theological Seminary, second highest in his class. Carl had for some years worked with high-school and college students as a minister in the Presbyterian Church, U.S. After discovering how dynamic high-school students became when trained with Campus Crusade for Christ methods and materials, Carl felt impressed of God to leave the pastorate and give leadership to the High-School Ministry of Campus Crusade for Christ. Carl and his wife, Sara Jo, believe intensely that God can use high-school students in a dynamic way today.

In Perry, Georgia, during one of Carl's week-long evangelistic youth crusades, 220 high-school students were introduced to Christ as their Savior. These students not only found Christ but they began to go everywhere telling other students and winning them to Christ. They learned how to share the basic gospel through the Four Spiritual Laws presentation, and went from community to community. They went to a little town approximately fifteen miles away, then to one twenty miles away, thirty, fifty and finally seventy-five miles away, sharing with other students the claims of Christ. When they returned from these witnessing experiences they shared the manner in which God had opened the door for them to present the gospel, thus reaching hundreds of other students for the Savior. Later, in Macon, Georgia, a city-wide youth effort involving most of the downtown churches resulted in 500 young people being reached for Christ.

I had known and had been impressed with Carl during our seminary days together, but had lost contact with him. Eventually, some of our staff, who had learned of God's blessing upon Carl's ministry and who had participated in some of his meetings, began to suggest that Campus Crusade for Christ should develop a high-school ministry. My first reaction was negative. Youth for Christ and Young Life and many local churches were already doing an excellent job of reaching high-school and junior high-school young people for the Savior. Our hands were full trying to reach college students and laymen. We had not begun to exhaust these areas of opportunity. Why should we assume the responsibility of working where there was at least some vital witness being given for the Savior. Several of the staff insisted, but I continued to be skeptical.

One of the most convincing arguments for launching a high-school ministry was the fact that in scores and even hundreds of situations college students would return home to the communities from which they had come, having been reached for Christ through Campus Crusade, and would seek to start Campus Crusade for Christ meetings among the high-school young people. Some groups were also starting as a result of the Lay Ministry. Thus, across the nation high-school Campus Crusade groups were starting unofficially. We had no control over them nor any opportunity to serve them unless we developed a special organizational program.

Carl came to Arrowhead Springs to discuss his interest in launching the high-school phase of our ministry. I suggested that, before we become involved in a high-school ministry, he meet with Sam Wolgemuth, president of Youth for Christ, and members of his staff; and with Bill Starr, head of Young Life, and members of his staff; and share the burden that was on his heart. If there was a place for Campus Crusade for Christ in the high-school ministry, and if it could be developed in such a way that there would be no conflict or competition with these other excellent organizations, I would reconsider. Carl met with these men of God whose one

106

concern is to help reach and disciple high-school students for Christ.

A short time later I invited Bill Starr and Sam Wolgemuth, together with some of their associates, to Arrowhead Springs to interact further concerning this project to reach high-school students for Christ. They were most warm and gracious. I remember Bill Starr's statement, which I believe expressed Sam Wolgemuth's thinking as well: "Carl and Bill, let me say to you that we are reaching perhaps only one percent of the high-school students of America. It would be naive of us to say that there is no room for Campus Crusade for Christ to reach high-school young people. We just ask that you cooperate with us, that you work with us, that you move carefully into what you are doing so as not to make unfortunate mistakes." We had prayer together and from that time on Campus Crusade began a great effort to expand this ministry to help reach some fifteen million high-school students.

We believe that God wants Campus Crusade for Christ to assume the role of serving the local church and other Christian organizations.

One of the great joys that I have is to meet at least twice a year for two days, have fellowship, study the Word of God, and pray together with four great men of God for whom I have a warm affection: Lorne Sanny, president of the Navigators; Dr. John Alexander, president of Inter-Varsity; Bill Starr, president of Young Life; and Sam Wolgemuth, president of Youth for Christ. We have great times of sharing and of fellowship together. These meetings have been invaluable in helping to keep communications open between organizations.

God has continued to bless the high-school ministry in a remarkable way. Within four years the staff has grown to one hundred fifteen serving thousands of students on scores of high-school campuses across the nation.

Because of the limited facilities of Arrowhead Springs and the fact that the ministry began in the South, Campus Crusade began holding high-school summer conferences at Covenant College in Lookout Mountain, Tennessee. After two summers they outgrew that facility and moved to Rollins College in Winter Park, Florida. With the expansion of Arrowhead Springs, West Coast conferences have been added. Last summer a total of 1,300 high-school students were trained. Now an Adult Academy of Youth Ministries and Biblical Studies has been started in Florida to train young laymen to be volunteer helpers in the high-school ministry and to train church leaders how to conduct a vigorous evangelistic high-school program.

The testimonies of high-school young people are exciting. They are filled with enthusiasm. Jim, a student from Florida whose football team had just won the state semifinal game, was interviewed by one of the largest newspapers in the state. "Before I became a Christian," he said, "I was a second-rate person, a second-rate student, and a second-rate athlete. Since I invited Jesus Christ into my life, I now have a reason to play and live, and that is for the glory of God. I think if people can see what I, as well as the rest of the team, have been able to accomplish with God's help, they will realize that He can do the same for them." It is of further interest to note that in addition to his many athletic awards Jim was voted outstanding player and won a scholastic award, which are the two top awards given to a player.

Jewell Peterson of Minneapolis, one of the first members of the high-school staff, says, "I remember when my sister and I got together to pray for a great outreach for Christ in her school. After our prayer meeting we made a list of all the students she could think of who she wanted to invite to a meeting in our home and called them and told them to attend our first meeting. Seventeen students turned out for our first meeting and we invited them back to our home the next week for hot chocolate, encouraging them to bring their friends. The next week fifty-six junior high students jammed into our home. The furniture had to be moved out to accommodate them all. That night as I shared the simple gospel message, several students invited Christ into their lives. As the Lord worked in the lives of these students, they wanted to share their faith with more and more students, so before the end of that year over 200 high-school students were reached with the message of Christ, and many responded by giving their lives to Him. Two of the boys who received Christ that year are now college students at Moody Bible Institute and both are preparing for fields of full-time Christian service. One of these boys has already been used of the Lord in leading scores of students to Christ. The students who became Christians began a daily prayer meeting before school

108

and some of them were known to walk three miles in 20°-below-zero weather to attend. The same students asked me to help them organize a beach witnessing program that summer, and though they were only eighth graders, they led several college students on the beach to the Lord."

The 15 million high-school students will soon be 16½ million by 1975 and they need to be reached and discipled for Christ. We invite interested readers to help us.

13

The Lay Ministry

One day as He was preaching on the shore of Lake Gennesaret, great crowds pressed in on Him to listen to the Word of God.

He noticed two empty boats standing at the water's edge while the fishermen washed their nets.

Stepping into one of the boats, Jesus asked Simon (its owner) to push out a little into the water, so that He could sit in the boat and speak to the crowds from there.

When He had finished speaking, He said to Simon, "Now go out where it is deeper and let down your nets and you will catch a lot of fish!"

"Sir," Simon replied, "we worked hard all last night and didn't catch a thing. But if You say so, we'll try again."

And this time their nets were so full that they began to tear!

A shout for help brought their partners in the other boat and soon both boats were filled with fish and on the verge of sinking.

When Simon Peter realized what had happened, he fell to his knees before Jesus and said, "Oh, sir, please leave us—I'm too much of a sinner for You to have around."

He was awestruck by the size of their catch, as were the others with him.

And his partners—too—James and John, the sons of Zebedee.

Jesus replied, "Don't worry! From now on you'll be fishing for the souls of men!"

And as soon as they landed, they left everything and went with Him.[1]

I do not know of a better illustration in the Scripture—as it relates to our lay ministry—than this passage, for there are multitudes of men and women who have been Christians for years, but who have never introduced anyone to Christ. They have fished for men, but their nets have never been filled. Their lives are fruitless, impotent, confused, carnal. And yet, when they learn how to walk in the Spirit and be controlled and empowered by the living Christ, when they learn how to share their faith simply and clearly, their nets begin to fill and soon they are ready to forsake all and follow Him. This has been demonstrated over and over again in the ministry of Campus Crusade for Christ, and especially in the lay ministry because so many who are associated with this phase of Campus Crusade for Christ's effort to help fulfill the Great Commission in our generation are older people who have experienced the spiritual drought so prevalent in the Christian community.

We are told, for example, that it takes 1,000 laymen and six pastors to introduce one person to Jesus Christ in an entire year. This is an amazing thought to me. There is little resemblance here between twentieth century Christianity and that of the New Testament.

There are thousands of illustrations I could give. One of the most exciting and dramatic is the story of Clarence Brenneman, an outstanding businessman in Oregon. Clarence is the son of a minister, was reared in a wonderful Christian atmosphere, and became active in the church while a very young man. Through the years he held many responsibilities in the church as a Sunday school teacher, Sunday school superintendent, and deacon. Because of his popularity and leadership in the church and his willingness to help in anything to do with the church, he was elected president of all the men in his denomination in the entire state. He was also elected to the board of trustees of one of the leading theological seminaries in America. And yet, as he said to me during one of his visits to Arrowhead Springs, "I've never led anyone to Christ." He had become a very successful businessman and was held in high esteem by the Christian and secular world of Eugene, Oregon, but, as he said, he had failed to achieve the most important thing—introducing another to the Savior.

I remember different contacts I had with Clarence and his lovely wife, Vida. They had attended for the first time a Lay Institute for

111

Evangelism at Arrowhead Springs. During that institute it was announced that as a part of the laboratory training all of us would go out to share our faith in the local community and put into practice the things we had been learning in the lectures and seminars. Clarence was petrified with fear. He suddenly remembered he had an urgent business matter that needed his attention in Eugene and caught the next plane home. But the Lord had already begun a wonderful work in his life and was not about to let him miss out on the greatest adventure a Christian can know. Later, Clarence attended another institute and when the opportunity was given to go to share our faith, Clarence went along, though still reluctant and filled with fear. At the first house he approached, he was overjoyed when a young housewife and her husband received Christ. This was the beginning for Clarence and Vida. Later, Clarence and fifteen other laymen joined with me in holding Lay Institutes for Evangelism in major cities around the world.

I remember an occasion when we were seated on the balcony of the Ambassador Hotel, looking out over Jerusalem and with our mind's eye following the path our Lord had traveled in that ancient city some 2,000 years before. Suddenly it occurred to me to ask Clarence, "What do you intend to make of your life?" In retrospect, I realize that was a rather unusual question to ask of a man who was already a leader in the church and one of the most prominent businessmen in his area. But as he shared with me later, that question caused him to rethink his whole commitment, and God used that question to cause him to change his plans. Today, he and Vida, after many other training sessions, have become involved in training other laymen. They have been used to introduce hundreds of others to the Savior. In addition to those whom they have reached personally, there are the thousands of laymen and students they trained who have in turn reached thousands for the Lord Jesus.

Here is an example of a man who fished long and hard for many years—weary in the service of the church—and his nets were empty. But then, in obedience to the commands to be filled with the Spirit and to learn how to share his faith, he soon filled his nets. As Clarence said to me since, "I begrudge even the small amount of time I now have to give to my business, for I want to make every moment of my life count in winning and in discipling men for

112

the Lord Jesus." Today, Clarence is regional director for the lay ministry in the northwestern states.

The lay ministry is a direct outgrowth of the campus ministry. As God continued to do a mighty work in the lives of thousands on many college campuses, laymen began to ask, "How do you account for the miraculous results of the ministry of Campus Crusade among students? You see as many students come to Christ on a single campus as we see in an entire city among the laymen. On many campuses there are hundreds of students coming to Christ and many of them become disciples within the year. Can't you give us the same kind of training you give your staff and students?"

Thus it was that I began to speak at many day-long Lay Institutes for Evangelism in various cities throughout the nation. From early in the morning until late at night, the basic messages and seminars on how to live the Christian life and share our faith in Christ more effectively were presented. Hundreds of laymen and pastors came for the entire day to hear this seminar presentation. Thus the lay ministry was born, and it has produced some of the most exciting results that we have seen.

For example, in one large city I was speaking at a meeting to which several hundred laymen and students had come from throughout the entire state, some as far as 500 miles. At the conclusion of one of my lectures a leading layman literally came running down the aisle with his pastor in tow. He said, "This is the greatest thing I have ever heard in my life. Today I have been liberated. I have been set free. I am now on twelve boards of various Christian organizations, including a couple in my church. I have been trying to serve God so diligently that I practically ignored my business and my family. Now you tell me that the Christian life is not what we do for God, but what we allow Him to do in and through us. You say the Christian life is a supernatural life, that no one can live it but Christ, and that this life is by faith through the power of the Holy Spirit. I have been trying to serve God in the energy of the flesh; I understand now why I have been so miserable and so unproductive!" He telephoned his wife, explained to her how he had made the discovery of being filled and controlled by the Holy Spirit by faith, and insisted that she come at once to join in the training. Even though she had made previous commitments, she canceled all her engagements and came.

113

That night at the banquet following my final lecture, they both stood to tell how their lives had been dramatically revolutionized that day through the new concepts they had heard, revolutionary concepts which caused them to redirect the course of their lives.

The day-long institutes for evangelism soon became week-long and spread to city-wide, encompassing hundreds of churches and thousands of laymen who responded to training. Seattle, Washington, was the scene of one of our largest institutes. Hundreds of churches cooperated in sending 1,200 delegates to receive training in how they could experience and share the abundant life in Christ. The results were most encouraging because these laymen and pastors returned to their churches aflame for Christ and determined to make their lives count for the Savior. Many of them are continuing to do a mighty work.

Among those making their lives count are Vern and Frances Thomas. Vern was an outstanding lumberman in the Northwest. He and his wife had committed their lives to Christ and were active in their church. They came to a Lay Institute for Evangelism at Arrowhead Springs, and, as we began to talk about the possibility of training people in the Seattle area, I asked Vern and Frances if they would be responsible for giving leadership to the organization and for the preparation of plans for an institute in their city. They accepted the challenge and went to work. Hugh Preston, an outstanding, dedicated young teacher in the area joined with them and others, and soon the dramatic results of their efforts were realized because the whole city was made aware that Jesus Christ is truly a living Savior. Today, Vern and Frances have filled their nets and have forsaken all and followed Christ. They have sold their business and their lovely home, and are now giving full-time direction to the lay ministry of Campus Crusade for Christ in the state of Washington.

I had just finished one of my lectures on the ministry of the Holy Spirit when a pastor approached me. He was rejoicing in the fact that he now knew he was filled with the Holy Spirit by faith, but he was also distressed by the fact that with all of his theological training and his many years of preaching, he had never once personally introduced one person to the Savior. He was rightly concerned. As we talked and prayed together, I felt impressed to ask him if he would like to be used of God that very day to introduce

114

someone to Christ. He looked at me in amazement as if to say, "How foolish! I've never led anyone to Christ in all these years. How could I possibly expect to lead anyone to Christ today?" I suggested that we pray together and then that he go door-to-door in the area where his church was located, using our Community Religious survey, and present the gospel through the Four Spiritual Laws. This he agreed to do. We asked God that He might honor his efforts. Imagine his elation and my joy when he returned that afternoon so excited he could hardly relate that in the very first home he visited, he met a nineteen-year-old student who was ready and ripe for the gospel and that upon the simple presentation contained in a *Four Spiritual Laws* this person bowed and prayed to receive Christ. Needless to say, this was a revolutionary experience for this young pastor.

The lay ministry began to experience phenomenal growth under the leadership of Roe Brooks, now our Massachusetts director for the campus ministry; later under Gordon Klenck, presently European director, the ministry continued to put down its roots. Then one day Howard Ball, an outstanding young businessman from Aurora, Illinois, and his wife, Barbara, appeared on the Arrowhead Springs scene. They had become interested because of the remarkable results they had seen among students who were being reached for Christ on campuses in their area, and they wanted their lives to count for the Lord also. Howard was concerned about the moral and spiritual decadence of our country. He was aware of the imminent threat of communism to our national security. He wanted to do something, but what could he do? He had come to Arrowhead Springs to explore possible answers to that question. Now, he found himself captivated by the most exciting challenge he had ever faced, that of fishing for men. He, too, filled his nets a year later, and he and Barbara sold their business and home in Aurora and moved to Arrowhead Springs to follow Christ. Soon after, Howard was appointed coordinator of the lay ministry and in 1968 was made the director. Under his leadership the lay ministry has continued to expand across the nation with a staff of more than 150 and a number of outstanding business executives and professional men who are now devoting most or all of their time in helping to organize and lead lay and pastors' institutes involving tens of thousands of laymen and pastors. Last year alone, more than 100,000 were trained in the various institutes for evangelism located throughout America.

Bill Menefee, president and chairman of the board of HomCare, a large international multi-million dollar chemical sales organization, was an active leader in his church. Yet his major concern was to place his products, one of the most famous of which is a cleanser, in every market of the world. He is well on his way to succeeding. However, something happened to Bill Menefee when he met Arlis Priest. He was challenged by his dedication to Christ and remarked, "Man, that fellow really gets through to me. I would like to know him better." Arlis was equally impressed with Bill Menefee and said to me, "You two should get together. Both of you think big; you both think in terms of the world. Bill Menefee wants to clean people up on the outside and you want to clean them up on the inside. You would have a lot in common."

Sometime later I did have the privilege of meeting Bill Menefee in Houston, Texas, the home of his international headquarters. In my honor he hosted a luncheon at which I had the opportunity to present the challenge of evangelizing and discipling the world for Christ in our generation. I was tremendously challenged by Bill from the very beginning. His enthusiasm and excitement for life were an inspiration to me. We decided to get together the following morning for breakfast before my departure for Los Angeles. At breakfast we talked about the Person of the Holy Spirit and how one can know the reality of His fullness and control by faith. We discussed the last words our Lord gave to His disciples following His resurrection and prior to His ascension: "But ye shall receive power, after that the Holy Ghost is come upon you: and ye shall be witnesses unto me." [2] I explained that the Holy Spirit was given not for the purpose of an emotional or ecstatic experience, but that we might live holy lives and be fruitful in our witness for the Savior. We prayed together; Bill claimed the fullness of the Holy Spirit by faith; and we both went on our ways rejoicing.

A few days later the telephone rang in my Arrowhead Springs office, and over the wire came the booming voice of Bill Menefee. "It works," he said, "it works. I have just had the opportunity of praying with a friend who received Christ." And there were many more in the days, weeks and months that followed. Indeed this became the practice instead of the exception as scores of men and

116

women were introduced to Christ through a businessman who had dreamed of saturating the world markets with his products. Now he has a greater vision, that of helping to take the good news of the gospel to the multitudes of the world until more than three billion, five hundred million people know of God's love and forgiveness in Christ.

Bill has not forgotten his business goals either and witnesses to the fact that his business is prospering more than ever. Today he is regional lay director for the southcentral United States, being responsible for helping to train thousands of laymen and pastors to be more effective in their lives and witness for Christ.

I was speaking at a Lay and Student Institute for Evangelism at Mount Hermon. Among those who were present were Henry and Beverly Schneider. Henry was an outstanding young engineer, not only managing his own engineering firm but serving also as a city chief engineer. Henry and Beverly had been reared in the church, and their knowledge of the Scriptures and their dedication to Christ were very obvious. But there was a restlessness in their hearts. They wanted to serve Christ more than they were able to do in the secular world. They came to inquire if there were a place for them on the lay staff of the Campus Crusade for Christ ministry. There was and is, and after two years Henry is now the southwestern states regional director for the lay ministry, and is being used to help train thousands of laymen and pastors from scores of churches. Henry and Beverly filled their nets and are helping other laymen to get their nets filled and to follow Jesus as well.

Harry Dickelman was a member of the prestigious Young Presidents organization, a select group of outstanding executives from across the United States who as presidents of their companies have achieved outstanding success before the age of 35. Harry and his wife, Gladys, became involved in the student phase of the Campus Crusade for Christ ministry and opened their home to staff and students and began to see some dramatic and exciting results from the investment of their time. They came to Arrowhead Springs and took special training for themselves. Soon their own lives had been transformed, and now they are directing the lay ministry of Campus Crusade for Christ in the Great Lakes region.

Only a few days ago a report came to me of how Harry had gone into Peoria, Illinois, called a number of the pastors together, laid before them a plan for training their laymen, and then held a brief pretraining program for the pastors and select laymen. A few months later, those who had received pretraining brought 1,700 of their fellow Christians to a week-long Lay Institute for Evangelism at which Harry and Gladys, together with their local staff, brought the lectures and seminars. Truly another example of what happens when one gets his nets filled.

Leroy Eger is one of those rare individuals who has the organizational ability to accomplish great things through knowing what to do and how to do it. As president of a nationwide organization with diverse investments, Leroy had achieved considerable success in the business world. More important, he and his wife, Lois, loved Jesus Christ and were active in their church. Yet, they were not seeing all that they thought God wanted them to see in terms of productivity. They wanted to be used of God in a greater way. This desire was fulfilled by participation in several Lay Institutes for Evangelism, and, finally, by Leroy's appointment as southeastern states regional director for the lay ministry. In this capacity, he supervises the lay institutes held in scores of churches and from which remarkable benefits have gone to the thousands who received this training.

One of the most exciting projects we have undertaken in the lay ministry is under Leroy's direction. Some time ago I received a telephone call from Art De Moss—a member of the Campus Crusade for Christ board of directors, an outstanding businessman and owner of several businesses—who was calling to express his concern for reaching the people of the world for Christ and, especially, on this occasion, the people in Haiti. His vision for business is exceeded only by his vision and his investments in many organizations and Christian projects to help influence multitudes for our Savior. Art and his charming wife, Nancy, devote much of their time to Christian activities designed to reach men and women of every strata of society for Christ. Their lovely home is the scene of frequent large gatherings of Philadelphia's leading citizens who are invited to enjoy their hospitality and at the same time hear the good news of Jesus Christ presented by nationally known Christian leaders in the business, professional and religious world. In his phone call Art stated that his foundation would like to experiment with us in training missionaries and national pastors for this type

118

of institute for evangelism training. Haiti was chosen for the pilot project and Leroy was asked to give on-the-spot direction. It was a two-week program. The first week involved training the missionaries so that they in turn could help train the national pastors the following week. Approximately fifteen missionaries arrived for training, and their enthusiasm, which at first was lukewarm, began to build throughout the week. Then, when they went out to share their faith in Christ in the local community, and scores of Haitians committed their lives to Christ, the missionaries were overwhelmed. They had never seen anything like this. As one missionary told me, "I saw more people come to Christ in that two-week period of training than I have seen in all the fifteen years of my missionary career in Haiti." The next week some 400 national pastors came and the miraculous blessing of the Lord continued. These pastors went out to share their faith in the fullness of the Spirit and in the course of that week saw more than 400 of their fellow countrymen commit their lives to Christ.

Three months later more than 500 national pastors, lay preachers and missionaries gathered in Haiti for basic and advanced training in how to experience and share the abundant life of Christ in the power of the Holy Spirit. More than 1,000 fellow Haitians were introduced to Christ during the days of training and a nationwide strategy for further training and evangelism was launched. Total evangelization of Haiti's seven million population by 1972 is the objective. With more than 400,000 professing Christians, Haiti has the possibility of being the first country in modern times to experience the fulfillment of the Great Commission of our Lord. I, along with more than one thousand trained pastors, lay preachers, and missionaries, am committed to that objective.

While in Haiti Art De Moss, his brother Dr. Robert De Moss, Leroy Eger, Curt Mackey my personal assistant, and myself spent considerable time interacting on how that same program which has proven so successful in Haiti could be launched in every country of the world. Curt has been a member of the staff for 15 years. His broad knowledge, together with that of his vivacious wife, Lois, enables them to make a vital contribution to the entire ministry.

If God continues to bless as He has, we anticipate that a dream and prayer of years' standing—that we might have the privilege of ministering to the 45,000 missionaries in the field—might be realized. I have always held the missionary in the highest esteem, and still do. I thought of the courage and dedication necessary to cause one to leave home and family for years, frequently for life; I thought of the time and talent and treasure given for the cause of Christ in remote and sometimes unproductive areas of the world. It was not until I began to visit the mission field, however, that I realized how much the missionary is a human being like myself—like other Christians—but with this one great difference: he is trying to serve Christ through cultural and language barriers that do not exist for Christians who seek to reach their own country-men. Thus, the needs of the missionary are infinitely greater than those of the average Christian. It was while I was in India with a group of laymen, holding a Lay Institute for Evangelism in New Delhi, that I began to realize that the missionaries represent one of the most strategic forces for spiritual revolution in the world and that if only they could experience as a whole the Lay Institute for Evangelism training that has proved to be so revolutionary, how much more could be realized for the cause of Christ around the world. Now, the Haitian project may well serve as the launching pad that will enable us to be a servant to the servants of multitudes around the world. What an exciting thought!

The lay ministry is dedicated to serving the local church. We are committed to the fact that the local pastor and laymen are the key to evangelizing their community, and if properly trained with an understanding of how to share their faith in the power of the Spirit, can be used of God in a revolutionary way, even as the first century Christians. Thus, lay institutes are held in hundreds of churches and in scores of city-wide efforts. The lay institute usually follows a certain format. A series of lectures are given covering such important and basic truths as how to be forgiven and cleansed of sin, how to be filled with the Spirit, how to walk in the Spirit, how to witness in the Spirit, and how to help fulfill the Great Commission in this generation. Each of these hour-long lectures is followed by an hour-long seminar of a practical nature designed to teach the students and laymen how to share Christ more effectively, what to say and how to say it, depending always upon the ministry of the Holy Spirit. Thousands of laymen and pastors have shared how these lectures have transformed their lives. One of the highlights of the week, so far as the women are concerned, is a program of social coffees and teas in the homes of the women who are taking the training. At these gatherings members of the staff and women who have been previously trained present the claims of Christ through testimony and a simple presentation of the gospel to groups of neighbors and friends of the trainees. This type of meeting is extremely productive, resulting in introducing literally thousands of persons to Christ.

I remember when we first began this program. Vonette had had considerable experience and success speaking in sorority houses on the college campus. It occurred to us that just as the young coeds had responded to the gospel years before, so now would their mothers and other women be responsive to a similar type of presentation. Vonette began to speak and the response was phenomenal. Often, most of the non-Christian women in attendance would pray to receive Christ. Vonette began to teach others, and the day came when one of the shiest of her students, who never dreamed that she would be able to give her testimony, gave a challenge that caused others to want to know the Savior. Through the power of the Spirit, Barbara Ball has overcome her shyness and is a radiant and effective speaker. Hundreds of women have fallen in love with her and her message introducing them to Jesus Christ.

Evangelistic breakfasts are also held in connection with lay institutes. During a Lay Institute for Evangelism at Lake Yale, Florida, I had the opportunity to speak to six mayors at a mayor's prayer breakfast in Orlando. There were some 250 of the leading citizens of Orlando in attendance, and after a simple presentation of the gospel, reminding these men of our Christian heritage and challenging them to give their lives to Christ, I closed my challenge with a prayer inviting them to receive Christ and then asking them to leave their names and addresses, if they had prayed to receive Christ and wanted additional information as to how they could grow. Forty-seven indicated that they had received Christ. I had prayed earlier that morning for fifty who would receive the Savior. Somehow, three must have failed to record their commitment, but I was confident that God was going to do a mighty work, which He did.

It was in the spring of 1966. We were meeting in Dallas, Texas, for a city-wide Lay Institute for Evangelism. More than 3,000 from hundreds of churches were participating. Dr. W. A. Criswell, pastor of the First Baptist Church, had asked me to speak in the Sunday morning service. I observed that two television cameras were focused on me and was told that the message was televised to an estimated 50,000 listeners each Sunday morning. Suddenly, it occurred to me that this would be the ideal time and an inexpensive way to record the Lay Institute for Evangelism lectures. So, within a matter of hours, the wheels were set in motion and a local filming company was on hand to film the five basic lectures. These were inexpensive films and not what one would consider to be particularly professional. We were not sure how effective they would be. As a matter of fact, I found it very difficult to believe that anyone would sit for an hour through a lecture on how to be cleansed of sin or one on how to be filled with the Spirit without losing interest. This was an inexpensive experiment that paid unbelievable dividends. Howard Ball informs me that more than half of all the laymen and pastors who receive lay institute training are trained through these films. I am still amazed at the success of the films, yet I rejoice that God has given us this opportunity of multiplying our outreach a hundredfold. More recently, during our city-wide Lay Institute for Evangelism in Sydney, Australia, which was held in the famous St. Andrew's Cathedral, another series of lectures was filmed and will soon be available. It is planned that the language of the various countries where the films are used will be dubbed in.

A long-distance call came from Billings, Montana. A group of pastors were concerned about bringing the gospel to their city of some 85,000 and the surrounding area with its population of 280,700. How could they do it? They felt they needed our Lay Institute for Evangelism training. Dr. Ron Jones who, with his equally dedicated wife, Mary Lou, had left a successful dental practice to give full time to the lay ministry, was sent to Billings with Clarence Brenneman to help them get organized.

In preparation for the Billings campaign, some seventy of the city's outstanding Christian laymen and pastors attended the Lay Institute for Evangelism at Arrowhead Springs. They came with a unique idea. Jack Dabner, one of the pastors, was extremely interested in television and in mass media as a means of communicating the gospel more effectively. He and the Billings committee sug-

122

gested that to supplement the regular lay institute I should prepare a series of lectures designed for non-Christians to be aired on prime time by local TV stations. Here was an opportunity to introduce additional thousands to our Savior. Five special thirty-minute messages were prepared for airing on the two local networks simultaneously. Also five fifteen-minute radio broadcasts were carried on five local radio stations simultaneously twice each day for five successive days. One thousand Christian laymen and pastors were trained during the Lay Institute and hundreds have already been introduced to Christ in the beginning days of a program designed to confront every citizen of the Billings area with the good news. The benefits of this total radio-TV saturation offers such great promise that I am persuaded that this use of the mass media will work in each of the 224 metropolitan areas of the nation. As a result, we anticipate the expansion of this concept of training and evangelism to work simultaneously in many similar situations.

For some time a number of denominational leaders have been carefully evaluating our Lay Institute for Evangelism program, and as a result have begun to use our training films and materials to train their own laymen.

How long does it take a student to learn to fly a plane through classroom instruction alone? This question was asked of a trainer. The answer: it can't be done. It is impossible to learn to fly a plane without getting into the cockpit and operating the controls while in flight. Classroom instruction is a part, but is never adequate to learn how to fly. How can one learn to introduce others to Christ? Through courses in personal evangelism? Never! It is not enough to know how to communicate. One must learn how to do by doing.

An integral part of our Lay Institutes for Evangelism is a laboratory training program. In less than twenty-four hours after the delegates arrive for an institute, they have already been told what to do, how to do it, and have spent a few hours in the field seeking to communicate their faith with others. The results are startling and revolutionary. Many, and I guess one could say most, go out on this first witnessing assignment with their fingers crossed. Many are frightened. As one woman said to me, "I won't go. I refuse to go." I assured her that she did not have to go, that it was strictly voluntary, and that she should not feel under any pressure to go.

She kept saying, almost as though she were in a state of shock, "I won't go. I won't go." And I kept assuring her that she didn't have to go. Finally, I suggested that maybe she should go with someone and listen. Reluctantly, and with a face white with fear, she left. Two hours later she returned bubbling with enthusiasm, overjoyed. She took my hand in both of hers and said, "I am so glad that you encouraged me to go. What a great loss I would have sustained had I not gone. My life was forever changed this afternoon when I saw God transform the lives of those who received Christ."

This is a dramatic illustration of hundreds of cases of men and women petrified with fear, never having witnessed for Christ before, thrust out to give the Holy Spirit a chance to use them. Over and over again we remind them that success in witnessing is simply sharing Christ in the power of the Holy Spirit and leaving the results to God. We ask them to say this aloud over and over several times in the course of the week, for there are so many who return discouraged and defeated if they don't see "results." We remind them that witnessing for Christ is our responsibility and privilege, but that it is the responsibility of the Holy Spirit to produce the fruit. Jesus said one must be born of the Spirit.

I have never introduced anyone to Christ and I never shall, though I have been privileged to participate with the Holy Spirit in sharing the good news of God's love and forgiveness in Christ in such a way that thousands have been drawn by the Spirit to the Savior. Though many do not have the privilege of introducing anyone to Christ on that witnessing assignment, they still come back rejoicing with radiant countenance, remembering that success in witnessing is simply sharing Christ in the power of the Holy Spirit and leaving the results to God.

An outstanding pastor of a large church of 1,500 members had come to Arrowhead Springs at the insistence of some of his laymen. While he was here his life was transformed. As he told his laymen in his first sermon after his return, "I actually received Jesus Christ as my Savior at Arrowhead Springs. I thought that I had been a Christian before, but apparently, like John Wesley of old, I was not a Christian."

As he recorded in his autobiography, John Wesley was a member of the Holy Club at Oxford, fasted and prayed every Wednesday

124

and Friday. He came to America as a missionary to the Indians in the hope that he might change his own soul. So it is in the lives of a good many laymen and pastors. They are good people, moral people, who believe in Jesus Christ but who have never experienced the new birth themselves.

This dear pastor on one witnessing occasion shared the claims of Christ as contained in the Four Spiritual Laws with fourteen people. Thirteen of these prayed with him to receive Christ. Truly, he was an excited man when he came back to make his report. Literally hundreds of individuals pray to receive Christ in the course of an afternoon of sharing Christ. The questions naturally arise: "Can these decisions for Christ be genuine? How can one be assured that those who prayed to receive Christ are sincere?" According to the eighth chapter of Acts, Philip spent only a few minutes with the Ethiopian eunuch. Jesus spent only a brief time with the woman at the well and with Nicodemus. The Spirit of God has created a hunger for our Savior within the hearts of multitudes of men and women throughout the world, and especially in the United States. Millions are ripe for the spiritual harvest, if properly approached in love and the power of the Holy Spirit. Seed that has long since been sown, watered and fertilized is now ready for harvest.

One of the reasons God has been pleased to use this ministry in such an effective way is that laymen have been taught to go forth with an expectant spirit, trusting the Lord, believing that God has already prepared the hearts of those to whom they go. They are not trying to convert people to their way of thinking or to their philosophy of life or even to their religion. They go to share the most wonderful, the most important news the world has ever received, the good news of God's love and His forgiveness in Christ Jesus. How can anyone say no if he really understands how much God loves him and how great is His purpose and plan for him! This is our conviction, and God has wonderfully blessed this expression of faith on the part of thousands who have received this training.

The Lay Ministry of Campus Crusade for Christ has a strategy designed to help local churches saturate each of the 176,000 precincts in the fifty states with the claims of Christ. Thus will we, using every means at our disposal and working with other servants of our Savior, fulfill the Great Commission in this generation, not only in the United States but in every country of the world.

It occurs to me there are many who may well be like Peter and John of old. They have fished for men for years; they are wearied and discouraged. They have never caught anything, never introduced another person to Christ. There is a solution. One needs simply to bow in prayer and ask the Holy Spirit to control and empower his life as he surrenders it to Christ. The Holy Spirit provides the ability to learn how to communicate Christ more effectively with others. Hundreds of Lay and Pastors' Institutes for Evangelism are held each year at Arrowhead Springs and across the nation to help laymen and pastors fill their nets and challenge them to forsake all and follow Him.

14

The Military Ministry

While visiting in Atlanta, Georgia, I was invited to address the congregation of a community church established by a local businessman with investments in real estate—a very gracious southern gentleman. He was Colonel John M. Fain, USAF, Retired. During World War II he had served on General Douglas MacArthur's 5th Air Force staff in the Pacific and now he was devoting most of his energies to introducing others to the Savior.

After I had spoken in his church, where a number of people responded by committing their lives to Christ at the invitation, Colonel Fain related how in the middle of the night he was awakened and felt strongly impressed of the Lord to ask me to start a new division of Campus Crusade for Christ for the military. He added that he would be available in whatever capacity the Lord would have him serve.

This rang a bell with me, for I had long been interested in reaching the military, and had on different occasions personally spoken at meetings for military personnel. I had always found servicemen very open to the gospel. Later, I suggested that Colonel Fain come to Arrowhead Springs to head up a military division of the expanding ministry of Campus Crusade for Christ. The military ministry now has a staff of approximately fifty and its outreach is worldwide. Among other things, it has distributed hundreds of thousands of Van Dusen letters and Four Spiritual Laws booklets in various army bases across the nation and around the world, especially in Viet Nam.

Just recently I heard a good example of the military ministry outreach. A brilliant young eye surgeon in Dallas, Dr. Jack Cooper, who had been chairman of our city-wide Lay Institute for Evangelism there, was visiting a hospital to provide medical treatment for a returning Viet Nam war casualty. While he was treating the soldier for an eye ailment Dr. Cooper asked him if he knew Christ as his Savior and if he had ever heard of the Four Spiritual Laws. The soldier reached into his shirt pocket and pulled out a dirty, somewhat tattered copy of the Four Spiritual Laws which he had received many months before on the front lines of Viet Nam. Through reading this booklet he had received Christ. Yes, he had heard of the Four Spiritual Laws and as a result his life had been changed.

Colonel Fain is the director of the Military Ministry of Campus Crusade for Christ. His wife, Barbara, is a gifted and popular Bible teacher. After World War II Colonel Fain served as a member of the staff of General "Hap" Arnold, chief of the U.S. Air Force, at headquarters in Washington, D.C., assigned to the training division. A member of a wealthy southern family, he was a playboy, but he came to know Christ through Scripture billboards along the highway admonishing him to repent and receive Christ. Though he had a praying Christian mother, he had lived far from God. At first he was infuriated by the signs, then was convicted and received Christ. A short time later his wife and daughter also became Christians. For several years they accompanied Colonel Fain in his evangelistic outreach.

There are over 3,000,000 men now serving our country in the armed forces. Approximately one third of these are now serving outside the United States. There are about 5,000,000 dependents (immediate family) of these servicemen. After sixteen years of cease-fire in Korea we still have 50,000 troops stationed there. Twenty-five years after the end of World War II, we have thousands of troops and their dependents stationed in Germany and Japan.

We have the promise of the Bible that we will continue to have wars and rumors of wars. With world conditions as they are we know that as one hot spot cools off there will be another one to take its place, requiring the presence of our armed forces personnel.

The dual concept of the Military Ministry is: (1) to present the claims of Christ to our men and women in the service, as well as

128

to their dependents, wherever they may be. Since our Armed Forces personnel are now in seventy-five countries of the world and some in areas now closed to missionary groups, it follows that the second phase of the dual concept is: (2) to train those men and women in the service to share the claims of Jesus Christ with others. The conference on military evangelism (COME) presents the same lectures which are given in the lay institute, and similar seminars adapted to military situations are presented. The trained Christian serviceman many times is the only source of the "abundant life" to the man in uniform, as well as to the national in whose country he may be stationed.

"Fantasia in Red, White, and Blue," a musical prose program, is the musical story of our flag. Designed to honor the service men and women of America and dedicated to the wives and mothers of our fighting men overseas, its purpose is fourfold: (1) to focus attention of citizens young and old on allegiance to our country; (2) to introduce men and women to the historical Person, Jesus Christ, and to tell them how one may know Him personally and live the abundant Christian life; (3) to assist military chaplains in their ministry to the military community; (4) to challenge commitment to Christian principles—to produce lives of purpose, power, and peace, and to become better citizens "for God and country." Featuring Jacqueline Fain Nims, the daughter of Colonel and Mrs. Fain, this program has been presented across the country with the governors of several states and the mayors of a number of cities either attending and/or proclaiming "Overseas Wives Day" within the state or city. "Fantasia" has been presented also on military installations, in high schools, and before civic groups. Hundreds of wives and mothers of servicemen have received Christ during these performances. André Kole, Campus Crusade for Christ's master illusionist, recently performed and spoke on a military base for the first time. Of his audience of 1,200 servicemen and their families, 300 made salvation decisions.

One staff member of Campus Crusade for Christ speaks each Sunday on a marine base in conjunction with the chapel program. He speaks to a group of about sixty-five marines and shares the Four Spiritual Laws. The response to this informal presentation has been such that as many as fifty, and never less than twelve have prayed to receive Christ at a single meeting.

A man in the army had become a disciplinary problem. His wife had left him; he had lost his "stripes"; and he had been informed by his commanding officer that if he got into trouble one more time, he would be processed immediately for discharge as an undesirable. At this point in his life he met a staff member of Campus Crusade who shared with him the Four Spiritual Laws. He prayed to invite Christ into his life, and his life started changing. Five months later he was named the outstanding enlisted man on the base and had earned back his "stripes"; he and his wife were talking about reconciliation.

A navy man who had already been processed for a dishonorable discharge was told how he could find Christ. He prayed to ask Christ into his life and God started the life-changing process. His commanding officer, when informed of his new life, called the Navy Department in Washington to have the discharge stopped. Two years later this man was a respected member of his outfit and doing a fine job in Viet Nam.

Lou Price, a member of the military staff, has personally introduced more than 1,000 servicemen to Christ in the last year. At least one was a general, commander of one of the largest bases in America. Most of Lou's ministry involves personal surveys followed by a presentation of the Four Spiritual Laws. Most of his time day and night is dedicated to introducing men to Christ.

Possibly nothing illustrates the effectiveness of this work so dramatically as the story of one changed life. Gary Taylor is a good case in point. He says: "All of my life I have searched for adventure. Flying jet fighters as a naval officer seemed to be the answer for a while—with the added bonus of prestige and material security. But my craving for real action wasn't filled by combat missions and world travel. So my wife, Carolyn, and I began a practical, realistic search for the most effective way to invest our lives for our Lord Jesus Christ. Exposure to Campus Crusade for Christ, to the changed and exciting lives of some staff couples, and our burden for the military gave us the answer. We have found the action we sought on the full-time Campus Crusade for Christ staff with the military ministry."

15

Athletes in Action

Athletes have played an important role in the ministry of Campus Crusade for Christ since its inception. In the early years all-Americans Donn Moomaw, Bob Davenport, Don Shinnick, world decathlon champion Rafer Johnson, and scores of others across the nation were active in the work.

The December 27, 1954 issue of the *Los Angeles Examiner* contained a full-page spread with testimonies of nine of UCLA's great team—the number one team in the nation that year. Nine of the eleven first stringers were active in Campus Crusade for Christ. Four of these received all-American honors during their college football careers. A portion of the article reads:

UCLA grid stars join the spreading of a religious crusade with the same contagious enthusiasm that sweeps the student body with the realization that the school has a winning team. Acknowledgement of God as their source of strength and comfort today is spreading from student to student and from campus to campus across the nation. The movement has a title, Campus Crusade for Christ, but it has none of the fanfare of old time evangelism. It has no organized membership, no high pressure campaign and nowhere has the movement taken root more firmly and flourished more rapidly than at the University of California at Los Angeles. No student can suspect there is anything Polly-anna in it when a man like Jack Ellina, all-American tackle, says to him in one of the informal meetings, usually held in a fraternity or sorority house at Westwood, "Christianity, if it is accepted by a person, does two things. First, it makes a difference in the daily living of an individual; second, it holds him sturdy in times of strife."

Take the words of another great all-American from the same 1954 UCLA team that the nation's coaches voted national champions. Says fullback Bob Davenport, "There is a greater team than our Bruin ball club or any other ball club, that is the great Christian team. The Bible promises anyone who follows the plays that Christ calls will experience a far greater life than this world can offer, plus an eternal life with Him."

In all, nine members of the UCLA football team are active in the Campus Crusade, which actually began some three years ago at the University of California in Los Angeles and has now spread to 151 college and university campuses. In addition to Ellina, a Christian Church member; and Davenport of the Brethren Church; there are Bob Long, end, all-coast second string, Congregationalist; Terry DeBay, quarterback, all-coast honorable mention, Community Church; Bob Heydenfelt, all-coast honorable mention, Nazarene; Primo Villaneuva, tailback, all-coast second team, Methodist; Clarence Norris, end, Baptist; Steve Palmer, center, Baptist; Don Shinnick, fullback, Baptist.

One of the first athletes to become active in the movement was Donn Moomaw, UCLA's all-American linebacker of 1952. He passed up a promising career in professional football to study for the Presbyterian ministry. In explaining his personal decision, Moomaw said, "I am playing on God's varsity now. The temporary thrills of athletic achievement and the applause of the crowds cannot begin to compare with the challenge and the thrills of sharing Christ with others."

Donn's influence for Christ is worldwide. I met one outstanding young businessman, a member of Donn's church, whose business takes him all over the world. "I was an atheist," he said, "until I met Donn Moomaw. Through his life and ministry I became convinced that Christ is the only way to God."

As the ministry of Campus Crusade for Christ grew, it became increasingly important that a special emphasis be given to the athletic ministry of Campus Crusade for Christ. As a result, the athletic ministry was expanded and in 1967 Dave Hannah was appointed to direct this phase of the campus ministry. During that year our Athletes in Action basketball team was formed to play many of the leading universities throughout the nation. The following year the Athletes in Action wrestling team was developed; later the weight lifting team was launched. I would like to say a word about each of these teams. But first, let me say a word about Dave Hannah.

Dave Hannah is a former football standout at Oklahoma State University and was recruited by the Los Angeles Rams for a professional football career. However, the Lord had other plans for Dave. An injury forced him to leave the Rams, and God led him to develop the Athletes in Action teams. He not only directs the athletic ministry, but also participates on the weight lifting team. He has been credited with a world record bent-arm pullover of more than 500 pounds. Dave had been looking for God during his high-school years, but failing to find any spiritual reality in his search he gave up and welcomed the classroom philosophy that Christianity was a nice ethical code, if you needed a nice ethical code.

"In my junior year I met the student body president from Colorado University, Swede Anderson. As we talked together he referred to Pascal's statement, 'There is a God-shaped vacuum in the heart of every man which cannot be satisfied by any created thing, but only by God the Creator made known through Jesus Christ.' I had tried filling this vacuum with football, good grades, fraternity life, girls, and cars. But these satisfied merely on a short-term basis. Swede shared how Christ alone had uniquely filled his life's vacuum, and I began to understand the difference between true Christianity and a religious philosophy or code of conduct. I saw how God personally—not just a code, but God—could actually live within me. That day I invited Jesus Christ into my life. He became the Lord of my life and definite changes became evident. The Bible came alive as I read it daily. I found Christians the most exciting people in the world to be around. I have discovered what Jesus meant when He said, 'I am the resurrection, and the life: he that believeth in me, though he were dead, yet shall he live.' [1] To me the Christian life is a great adventure, far more exciting than the most dramatic athletic contest."

133

The Athletes in Action basketball team represents a new kind of game. The players make up a top amateur team, but they are committed to using their basketball skill to spread the Christian message. During the last two years our basketball team has won 37 and lost 45 games, an outstanding record when one considers that all the games were played on the road against some of the best teams in the nation. Some of our outstanding victories came against Bradley University, North Texas State, University of Southern California, University of Oregon, Brigham Young University and Kansas State University. The men who play on our basketball team are dedicated to making an impact for Christ wherever they go. Many have declined opportunities for high paying jobs to invest their lives in this worldwide ministry. Their purpose is to present Jesus Christ and to call America back to a solid faith and the Christian principles upon which this country was founded.

Fred Crowell, head coach of the Athletes in Action basketball team, is a native of Anacortes, Washington, and a graduate of the University of Idaho, where he earned his B.S. in physical education and a master's degree in education. He was freshman basketball coach at Idaho University in 1964–65 and then moved on to become head coach at the University of Alaska. From there he came to Arrowhead Springs to help organize our Campus Crusade basketball team, and has been head coach since the team was formed. Fred himself was introduced to Christ through the ministry of Fred Dyson, our Campus Crusade for Christ director in Alaska at that time.

Ray Burwick is assistant basketball coach, and prior to coming to Campus Crusade for Christ he was coach and athletic director of Cascade College in Portland, Oregon. Ray is a native of Dickinson, North Dakota, and graduated at Northwest Nazarene College in 1962. He earned his master's degree in education at Oregon State University in 1965.

The wrestling team was launched in 1967 with an outstanding group of wrestlers touring Japan. Last year, under the leadership of John Klein, they compiled a most enviable record: 11 wins, 4 losses, and 2 ties. Eleven of their opponents were in the nation's top twenty teams. Eleven members of our Campus Crusade for Christ wrestling team were all-Americans.

John Klein's first contact with Campus Crusade was at the University of Minnesota during the spring quarter of 1964, when his roommate and Gary Olander, a staff member, asked John to attend a Bible study.

John says, "It was at that meeting that I was presented with the simple truth of how to become a Christian. I trusted Christ at that meeting . . . Christ now means everything to me. I want to follow His plan for my life."

Our weight lifting team was organized following the 1968 Olympic Games when Russ Knipp joined the staff of Campus Crusade for Christ. Russ was winner of the Pan American Games for his weight class in 1967 and Weight Lifter of the Year in the United States the same year. He was a member of the 1968 U.S. Olympic Team and has set twenty-three national and American records and nine world records. He recently returned from Poland where he won the gold medal in the press for the United States. He attended Kendall College in Chicago.

Russ Knipp recalls, "Throughout my life I made the same search that everyone makes because he is human—the search for satisfaction and happiness. The means I chose was the glory that I believed came with being a world champion. I spent eight years giving everything I had in me to being a world caliber lifter. But setting twenty-three national and nine world records gave me no permanent happiness or satisfaction; there was always the next medal or the next world record to fight for. My world was empty and meaningless, in spite of all the glory. The athletic ministry of Campus Crusade for Christ heard of my efforts and asked me to visit them at their headquarters. I thought a short break in training for the Olympics would do me good. At Arrowhead Springs I saw something in the people—a deep happiness—that I knew I didn't have and knew I wanted. It was Christ. Therefore, I asked Him to come into my life. Soon the whole world took on a new perspective. All worry and burden was gone. I felt a definite change in my life. I then wanted to go to thousands of people to reach them, not with a title, but with a message of great joy. This joy comes from the realization of God's great love for us and from the love we can have for each other when Christ is in our hearts." Today, as a member of American Athletes in Action wrestling team, Russ Knipp shares his faith daily for Christ.

Wes Neal, another member of the team, is a graduate of San

135

Fernando Valley State College in social science, and of Pacific Lutheran Seminary. He set school records in the shot-put and discus and placed second in the California weight lifting championships.

Russ and Wes began putting on weight lifting programs in high-school assemblies, and the reception to their demonstration and presentation of the gospel was so great that we decided to develop a team which would expand to tour the nation. So, Dave Hannah and his wife, Elaine, and Alan Nagel joined the team in the fall of 1969 for a coast-to-coast speaking tour of high-school assemblies. The team has performed and presented the claims of Christ before approximately 200,000 students this year. Already more than 12,000 students have received Christ this school term through their influence. These men are outstanding competitive lifters as well as adept and forceful speakers. So they also provide valuable weight lifting and training hints.

Pat Matrisciana, former outstanding athlete at the University of Washington, handed me a November 10, 1969, issue of *Sports Illustrated* containing a picture of Steve Owens, Oklahoma University's great football star, who had just been awarded the Heisman trophy. "Meet your great-grandson," Pat said. In response to my puzzled expression, he said, "I had the privilege of introducing Steve to Christ when I was directing the ministry of Campus Crusade at Oklahoma University three years ago." Now I understood what he meant—Steve Owens, Bill Bright's great-grandson—he was speaking spiritually, of course.

This spiritual chain reaction began ten years ago, for it was then that I had the opportunity to introduce Fred Dyson to Christ while he was a member of the crew at the University of Washington. Fred was militantly opposed to Christianity, called himself an atheist and would have nothing to do with Christians—with one exception.

He was interested in a beautiful young Christian coed whom he had traveled from Seattle to Houston, Texas, to visit. She brought him to a meeting at which I was speaking at Rice Institute. Following the meeting we talked for a couple of hours about the intellectual basis for the Christian faith, the reasonableness of the Christian life, and Fred's need to make a commitment to Christ. Finally, when his questions were answered Fred said, "I am ready

136

to pray. I would like to receive Christ right now." It soon became apparent that Christ had changed Fred's life, for he immediately began to share his new-found faith with others and among the first whom he introduced to Christ was Pat Matrisciana, a fellow athlete at the University of Washington. A couple of years later, upon the completion of their college degrees and after considerable maturing spiritually, they both joined the staff and Pat was assigned to Oklahoma University where he had the opportunity to introduce many to Christ. Among them was one of the great athletes of our time, Steve Owens.

Over the years, many other athletes have come to know Christ through our work. Most recently were two boys on the great 1969 Arkansas football team.

Approximately 50 million people saw the University of Texas Longhorns defeat the Arkansas Razorbacks by the narrow margin of one point in the 1969 "game of the year." It was a thrilling game attended by many celebrities, including the President of the United States, who afterward awarded the winning team a plaque for being the number one team in the nation. What most people do not know is that there were several Christians on both teams, Christians active for Christ and active in the ministry of Campus Crusade for Christ. Our campus director at the University of Arkansas, Don Meredith, reported:

"Two summers ago, after our first three months on campus, Gordon McNulty and Terry Don Phillips became the first athletes from Arkansas to attend a conference at Arrowhead.

"That next fall Gordon and I began to spend hours together. Because he was a team leader, I began to feel at home in the Wilson Shard House (athletic dorm). In the spring, Dave Hannah and Larry Griffith came to Arkansas to speak at our spring conference. Dave conducted a team meeting with about fifty players. From that meeting we started an action group that ended in June with eight key players coming to Arrowhead.

"Two players, Gordon and Cliff Powell, stayed half the summer and worked on summer staff. It was now obvious that the 1969–70 school year would be exciting because of the way the whole state of Arkansas looks up to the Razorback football players. So, while at Arrowhead, I began to challenge Gordon and Cliff to pray about doing something big in the fall.

137

"After several days Gordon came up with the idea of writing ABC television to see if some of the players could share their faith on national television just before the Texas-Arkansas football game. ABC liked the idea and made the film, though in the end it was not aired. Still the experience had a fantastic effect on the young men. It gave real purpose to them and greatly matured their prayer life. They took real leadership in College Life and in talking to other students about Christ. Five other athletes have accepted Christ this fall and many others are interested.

"Bill Montgomery, one of the athletes who accepted Christ in October, had such a change in his life that his girl friend asked my wife, Sally, how she could know Christ, too. After Shari accepted Christ she was immediately responsible for two other Delta Delta Delta sorority girls accepting Christ. Bill also started an action group that God is using in the Sigma Nu fraternity.

"All in all though, the most significant thing that really indicated the growth of these athletes is the testimony Gordon, Bill, Cliff, and Bill Burnett gave the morning after the loss to Texas. Over 600 students were moved as these men shared, 'Not my will, Lord, but Yours.'"

Another great 1969 team was the University of Missouri Tigers. Rick Duwe, Campus Crusade for Christ director for the state of Missouri, has had a remarkable ministry with the athletes on that great university campus, and especially with the football players. Rick said, "The men meet Saturday mornings before each game for Bible study, prayer, and discussion. The group started with six and has mushroomed to seventeen. Three of the men met Christ because of the witness of the group. Several team members have spoken of their faith in Christ to churches and civic groups around the state. Many newspaper articles have been written about their spiritual lives and witness. Most of the players credit the success of the season to the spiritual emphasis established by several of the team's leaders. They feel that the Lord has given them a special love for each other, particularly between blacks and whites. Last spring the racial situation on the team was somewhat tense, but a change has taken place since last year because the leaders and best players on the team have been Christians. Most of them Spirit-filled, and as a result there is an unselfish spirit that affects the whole team. Joe Moore, a black, told me, 'I don't look at guys like Terry McMillan and Jerry Boyd as guys I played ball with in college, but as buddies that I love.' Even after their only loss this season to Colorado, the Christians were praising the Lord after the game. Several of the players come over to the house on the Thursdays before most of the games for an hour or so of prayer. These have been powerful and enriching times of fellowship together."

Thousands of other athletes on hundreds of high-school and college campuses are active in the Ministry of Campus Crusade for Christ. Many of these have dedicated their lives to helping to change the world. All athletes—high school, college, professional and those who enjoy athletics from the bench—can have a part in helping to inspire, challenge, recruit, and train tens of thousands of athletes for Christ. Athletes are usually held in high esteem by their fellow students and colleagues, and can be effective witnesses for Christ when they learn how to live radiant, dynamic, Spirit-filled lives.

Members of the Athletes in Action teams conduct championship conferences to teach athletes how they can have an impact for Christ. Held at Arrowhead Springs and at other training centers, these conferences include physical conditioning, Christian films, lectures, clinics, and recreation designed to help every athlete develop both athletically and spiritually.

16

Multiplying the Message

Bob George, his wife, Amy, and their children, were seated in their comfortable living room watching a television program. This program was not the usual affair. There was something different about it. It was called "Campus Crusade—A New Kind of Revolution." It featured Pat Boone; Paul Stookey of Peter, Paul and Mary; Bobby Vee; the New Folk; a number of students; and myself. The hour-long color television special sponsored by Campus Crusade for Christ was a fast-moving, action-packed, dramatic presentation, involving contemporary music, active interaction between a number of Christians, non-Christians, militants, blacks and whites as they shared their views concerning sex, dope, university life, government, and a number of other relevant issues. It concluded with a message that Jesus Christ is our only hope, and invited the viewer to commit his life to Christ and to write Arrowhead Springs for a book entitled *Revolution Now!* for information in regard to how one can get involved in the great spiritual revolution.

Bob and his family were greatly moved. This is what they had been looking for all of their lives. Bob and Amy were active in a local church where he was an elder, a member of the building committee and of a few other responsible boards, but they had never made the wonderful discovery of knowing Christ personally. This was their night of decision.

As soon as the program was over, they wrote to request a copy of *Revolution Now!* so they could know more about how to help change the world. Twenty-five hundred similar letters came from

140

the estimated one million viewers. All of those who wrote in from Los Angeles were invited to Arrowhead Springs for a special follow-up meeting at which I spoke. I concluded my remarks to these visitors with a challenge for them to commit their lives to Christ, and closed with a prayer of invitation to receive Him. If any one had any questions, I was available to talk to him personally.

Bob immediately expressed his interest in receiving Christ personally. After we had prayed together, I asked him about his wife. "I want her to become a Christian, too," he said, and a short time later Amy and I were also in prayer. Bob and Amy went away rejoicing over the discovery of their new life in Christ.

This was only the beginning. They began to share their faith and have seen a number of their friends, business associates and employees receive Christ. Bob is a very successful young businessman in the southern California area.

Later, Bob's father became ill with cancer, and he and Bob's mother came to California to visit. Bob wanted them to know Christ. Even though they were good, wonderful church members, he was sure they did not know the Savior. He called and asked if he could bring them to Arrowhead Springs for a personal conference. They came and we had a delightful chat. Since they had been reared in the church, they knew the language and gave every indication to me that they were Christians. I gave them a copy of *Revolution Now!* and later the father reported to Bob that through the reading of the book he had committed his life to Christ. Shortly thereafter he went to be with the Lord, and Bob used the opportunity during the illness and the funeral service that followed, to pray with a number of his relatives, who received Christ.

In the meantime, over a four-month period, Bob was involved in three specialized lay institutes for evangelism as he sought to learn everything he could about reaching others for the Savior and helping to change the world.

One day following a training session, he said, "I have a great idea. Who is following up all the rest of the 2,500 people who wrote in from the Los Angeles area in response to the same television program which I saw?" I explained to Bob that we have a very special follow-up program and that each individual was receiving a series of twelve Bible correspondence letters, together with other materials to help them commit their lives to Christ and to grow in the faith. Because of limited personnel we were not able to visit them personally. Whereupon Bob said, "I have felt strongly impressed of the Lord in the last few days that I should be personally responsible for following up all of these other 2,500 people. Would you allow me the privilege?"

I was overwhelmed. Here was a young man who was only four months old as a Christian. Yet, because he had been exposed to vital training he was already aware of how to walk in the Spirit and to share his faith, and had been used of the Lord to introduce many to Christ. Now he was concerned about the personal follow-up of those who, like himself, were inspired to respond to the television program, "Campus Crusade—a New Kind of Revolution." We gave him that assignment and he immediately began to organize a number of people whom he has introduced to Christ. Working with other friends of Campus Crusade for Christ in the Los Angeles area, they are following up personally the other 2,500 people who responded when he did. Bob is typical of millions of Americans waiting to be reached and discipled for Christ, waiting to become a part of the great movement to help change the world. What better way to reach them than through the mass media?

The mass media of communications—newspapers, radio, motion pictures, and television—have made a tremendous impact upon society. They influence public opinion, help mold character, and have a great impact on almost every phase of human existence. Computers have invaded and pervaded the center of all of our personal lives and must be utilized for Christ. As Christians, there is very little doubt that we should use these media for the proclamation of the gospel.

Dr. S. I. Hayakawa reports that by the time a youngster reaches eighteen years of age he will have spent 22,000 hours in viewing television, nearly twice the amount of hours he will have spent in school. A national average for all ages is six and one-half hours of television viewing per home per day. It is estimated that 84 percent of what we remember is received through the eye, whereas 12 percent of what we remember comes through the ear and the balance through the other three senses. Obviously, television, films and other audiovisuals, must be utilized by Christians to communicate the claims of Christ effectively to the entire population of the world.

Utilization of the mass media is a vital part of the world wide strategy of Campus Crusade for Christ. For example, our mass media ministry is divided into four major departments: publications, audiovisuals, radio and television, and correspondence.

All of these are under the direction of Ron Wormser, who is well qualified by training and experience to give leadership in this, one of the most strategic facets of our world-wide ministry. Ron studied for the ministry, received his B.A. and M.A. and did further graduate and seminary work. Following this period of study, he was assistant pastor and youth director of a large church for six years, associate director of a daily evangelistic radio broadcast for five years, and pastor of a growing suburban church for five years. Then one day Ron heard a member of the Campus Crusade for Christ staff share how men eagerly respond to the message of Christ when they understand how to invite Christ into their lives. Ron found it difficult to believe this because he had not found this true in his own experience. Yet, following a series of events, he and his wife, Carole, found themselves at Arrowhead Springs attending a Lay Institute for Evangelism. Ron reports that this was the turning point in their lives. It was here that they learned how to experience by faith the fullness and control of the Holy Spirit and how to communicate their faith more effectively. Because of what the training meant in their own personal lives, they realized what it could mean in the lives of others across the country. About halfway through the week of training at Arrowhead Springs, God impressed upon Ron and Carole that He wanted them to be a part of the worldwide ministry of Campus Crusade for Christ.

Upon completion of their application, and training, they were assigned to the lay ministry and, approximately a year later, Ron became the national coordinator for the lay ministry under the direction of Howard Ball. For two years he served faithfully and effectively in that role. Then one day as I was praying for someone to give leadership to our publications ministry, it suddenly occurred to me that Ron Wormser was the man. I had had opportunity to work closely with him in the editing of many articles, and Ron knew my mind and shared my concerns. I felt that he, more than anyone I knew, was the one who could give direction to this very important phase of the ministry, for which I personally had been responsible for almost eighteen years. Accordingly, I asked

143

Ron to assume the responsibility for directing the publications ministry and later the mass media ministry.

Our publications have been used of God to reach many millions of men and women in many parts of the world with the claims of Christ. One of the most significant of these is *Collegiate Challenge,* a quarterly publication designed especially for the non-Christian collegian. Bob Cording, has given creative direction to this magazine as the assistant editor and art director for five years, and is presently doing special projects as an associate staff member. Judy Downs, who has been on staff for four years, not only serves as copy editor for the *Collegiate Challenge,* but gives leadership to the writing team of the publications ministry. It is estimated that it is read by more than half a million readers on hundreds of campuses across the nation. Thousands of students have made commitments to Christ through the influence of this magazine and hundreds of stories could be told. For example, one young woman picked up a copy of *Collegiate Challenge* in her sorority house and was reading it when a member of the Campus Crusade staff dropped by, saw her reading it and began to chat. As they talked together, the young woman received Christ. Later, as she matured in Christ, she joined the Campus Crusade for Christ staff and is now being used in a vital way to introduce many others to the Savior.

A leading and very effective pastor in America said to me one day that he looks forward to receiving his copy of *Collegiate Challenge* more than any other Christian publication because it is filled with the kind of content he likes to use in his sermons. *Collegiate Challenge* won the "Periodical of the Year" award at the Evangelical Press Association Convention in 1968, plus first place in the general magazine category and other awards in specific areas. On many campuses members of the staff and Christian students give copies to students at random, ask them to read and make an appointment to talk about Christ the following day. They have found that a simple reading of the magazine has prepared the hearts of many to receive Christ.

Athletes in Action is a magazine designed for the athletic world. Edited by Gail Habluetzel, a talented writer, and designed by Weldon Hardenbrook (head of our art department), it contains a number of secular articles featuring different sports and training

144

tips. Woven into these articles are the testimonies of outstanding Christian athletes with appropriate explanations of how one can become a Christian. Thirty thousand copies are printed quarterly, though as many as 250,000 have been printed of special issues, and the response on the part of coaches and athletes has been most encouraging. *Student Action* is a quarterly newspaper that has a circulation of more than 500,000. This paper is especially designed to communicate to the student information concerning Christ and contemporary issues. The college campuses today are flooded with all kinds of radical and pornographic literature. To counteract the evil, brainwashing technique influencing such a large segment of the university world, it is the objective of Campus Crusade for Christ to publish several million copies of *Student Action* each month of the school term. Exciting results have been reported from its distribution. Often as many as 15,000 copies are distributed on a single campus in a single morning by students who have stationed themselves at the entrance to university campuses. Through this medium alone, thousands of students have indicated their desire to commit their lives to Christ and to become a part of a spiritual revolution.

Campus Crusade also publishes a newspaper especially designed for pastors, laymen and others who are interested in the overall worldwide ministry of Campus Crusade for Christ. It carries the stories of pastors, laymen and students who have been awakened and revitalized for Christ because of the various training programs of Campus Crusade. It also includes articles that challenge the reader to a greater commitment to the Savior and to His command to help fulfill the Great Commission in our generation, plus testimonies of what God has done in various churches and in the lives of individuals. This newspaper is also published quarterly, with 250,000 copies each issue.

The book, *Revolution Now!,* which contains the basic messages and content of the Campus Crusade for Christ training, was published in July, 1969. By February, 1970, 118,000 copies had been ordered and committed for distribution.

The Van Dusen letter is one of the most popular pieces of evangelistic literature in our literature program. More than 10 million copies have been distributed in most major languages of the world. The name Van Dusen is fictitious. Originally it was written to a businessman who had expressed an interest in knowing Christ. As a result of a personal conversation which I had had with him, he had asked me to come to see him to discuss the matter. Since he lived in New York and I lived in Los Angeles, and it was not possible for me to visit him personally, I wrote him a letter explaining the basic facts concerning Christ and the Christian life. After mailing the letter, it occurred to me that this was the kind of a letter that I would write to almost anyone whom I wanted to introduce to our Savior. So several thousand copies of the letter were mimeographed with the fictitious name of Van Dusen replacing the name of the friend to whom I had orginally written. These mimeographed copies were sent to members of the staff to be used in their work with students. The response was so encouraging, in some cases even phenomenal, that we decided to start printing them. The rate has continued to accelerate and today millions of copies are being used all over the world. On the basis of the many experiences which have been brought to our attention, it is reasonable to believe that thousands of men and women are coming to know Christ, as a result of reading this letter.

An estimated 25,000,000 copies of the Four Spiritual Laws booklet and 10,000,000 Van Dusen letters have been printed and distributed in most major languages of the world. *The Ten Basic Steps toward Christian Maturity,* a Bible study series, and numerous other booklets and articles have received widespread distribution among college and high-school students, as well as adults and pastors.

The rapidly expanding audiovisual department has experienced phenomenal growth and expansion. It is under the direction of Bill Strube, former insurance company president, and his wife, Elizabeth. They are ably assisted by Chuck Younkman, a former college professor and his wife Jerri. Films, filmstrips, tapes, records, and other audiovisuals are designed to inspire, instruct and train staff, students and laymen in the basic messages and philosophy of Campus Crusade. They include such films as "Bal Week," which tells the story of the beach ministry; "Berkeley—A New Kind of Revolution," which records the week-long Berkeley convention; "In Our Generation," which tells the story of our overseas ministry; and "Come Help Change the World," which tells the story of Campus Crusade for Christ; the *Lay Involvement* film, which tells the story of how our churches can experience a spiritual awakening through the Lay Institutes for Evangelism; and several films which feature my lectures about "How to Experience a Cleansed Life," "How to Be Filled with the Holy Spirit," "How to Walk in the Spirit," "How to Witness in the Spirit," and "A Strategy for Fulfilling the Great Commission in Our Generation," and "How to Love."

Many people are using their time twice as they take advantage of the purchase and rental facilities of our tape library. With the compact, inexpensive, playback equipment now available, people are finding that they can easily listen to tape recordings while driving, working in their homes or offices, enjoying a time of relaxation, etc. There are more than 250 titles available on subjects ranging from the ministry of the Holy Spirit, training for evangelism and family living, to evangelistic messages and a series of studies of several books of the Bible.

The radio and television ministry of Campus Crusade for Christ is faced with a dramatic era of expansion. Director Gene Vurbeff, for many years a professional radio and television producer, and his wife, Robin, joined staff four years ago. Campus Crusade for Christ's "Challenge for Today" is heard on approximately 180 radio stations each week. Thousands of viewers have responded to our hour-long TV special, "Campus Crusade—A New Kind of Revolution." A special half-hour weekly color TV series has been projected for 1971. It is estimated that through this series several million viewers will be challenged each week with the claims of Christ and the opportunity to help change the world.

A special correspondence department has been developed which is now under the direction of Larry Rennick, who with his wife, Toya, came from a successful business and management career to assist in this strategic effort. It is the purpose of this ministry to communicate with tens of thousands of men and women, students and laymen, who are introduced to Christ through the ministry of Campus Crusade. Staff members and friends of Campus Crusade are encouraged to forward the names of those who respond to the claims of Christ through the various personal contacts and group meetings across the nation. Each individual receives a series of twelve Bible correspondence follow-up letters. Each of these letters is personalized and encourages the reader to answer certain questions that relate to basic Christian doctrine and the practical phase of his daily Christian experience. Enclosures assist in a better understanding of the Christian life. In addition, the thousands, and ultimately millions, of listeners to the various radio and television programs will be followed up through correspondence and encouraged to become a part of the Great Commission army and to help fulfill the Great Commission in this generation.

Early this year, Dr. Walter Judd invited me to participate in a meeting attended by several Christian leaders in Washington, D.C. Among those present were a number of congressmen and leaders in various fields of endeavor, including communications. One of the men announced that we were now at a point of break-through in communications so that a single message could be televised via satellites to a billion people at one time. Immediately my mind raced as I thought of how this one message *must* be the good news of God's love and forgiveness in Jesus Christ. Surely, as Christians, we must take advantage of this remarkable breakthrough at the earliest possible date to tell the people of the entire world that God loves them and has a wonderful plan for their lives that was revealed through His personal visit to this planet in the Person of the Lord Jesus. A few days after my return from Washington I read in the *Los Angeles Times* that 500,000,000—yes, five hundred million—people watch the popular western, "Bonanza," each week. That is amazing to me! A purely secular program, designed for entertainment alone, is being shown to 500,000,000 people around the world. Also, I learned that more than 600,000,000 people throughout the world saw our astronauts land on the moon. This number represents more than one-seventh of the world's population. Surely, the Great Commission can be greatly accelerated through the utilization of the mass media.

17

All Things to All Men

The Apostle Paul was a great fisher of men. Through every honorable means he sought to introduce others to Christ. He stated his successful methods in I Corinthians 9:22, "I am made all things to all men, that I might by all means save some." [1] He went where they were. He met them on their own level. He was "wise as a serpent" in arresting their attention. Everywhere he went he talked about Christ to all who would listen, warning them, and teaching them. He wanted to present each one to God, perfect because of what Christ had done for each of them. And he was amazingly successful.

Let me tell you of some of the "all things" Campus Crusade for Christ does to "save some" and of the thrilling success God has given through our special projects.

André Kole, billed as America's leading illusionist, is also recognized as one of the leading inventors of magical tricks. On the stage he does everything from making people appear and disappear to sawing in two his attractive wife, Aljeana. André is a special representative of the Campus Crusade for Christ staff. He uses the fantasy of magic to gain a hearing for presenting the reality of Christ. "Throughout the world," he says, "I find more and more people who are turning to the world of fantasy in their vain attempt to find reality. During the past twenty years as a professional magician I have lived in a world of fantasy and illusion, but I discovered that Jesus Christ is no illusion. He is a reality and we can know Him in a personal way." As a young, successful businessman and entertainer, André Kole became a Christian, but it was not until he met Elmer Lappen, director of Campus Crusade for Christ in Arizona, and began to attend leadership training sessions there that he began to grow. He accompanied Elmer on personal evangelism appointments, at which he first observed and then experienced in his own witness the hunger for Christ in the hearts of students for Christ. God called him from an outstanding career, a dual career of business and illusion, to serve Him on the college campus as a member of our full-time staff. Since joining the staff, André's appearances have taken him to all fifty states and to forty-three countries on five continents. He has appeared on nationwide television in thirty countries and has made numerous appearances before presidents, generals, and other public officials throughout the world. During one school term he presented the claims of Christ to an average of one million people each week on television and to live audiences. An average of approximately 1,000 people a week pray to receive Christ as a result of his various meetings. Another thousand or more inquire how they can become Christians or express their desire to know more.

I asked André why he was willing to be away from his wife and family for long periods of time, and to give up a successful business career and the chance of being billed as one of the greatest illusionists in history at great remuneration. He replied, "I am constrained by the love of Christ and the desperate urgency of the hour to help bring America and the world back to God, and to help change the world. All good is good, but to do a lesser good when it is possible to do a greater good is sin. It is not the good itself but the doing of the lesser that is sin."

Among the thousands who have come to Christ through André Kole's ministry are some who have made very interesting comments. A student leader in Taiwan said, "Mr. Kole, when you mentioned that most people are laughing on the outside and crying on the inside, you described me perfectly. Not only is this a picture of my life, but of the life of every student I know on this campus. I only wish I had heard you a week ago or even a day ago." And: "You saved my life tonight. If I had not heard this message tonight I would have committed suicide"; "I have been a Christian for eleven years but I closed Christ out of my life when I came to college. About a year ago I attempted suicide. I saw nothing worth

150

living for. Since then I have been seeing a psychiatrist, but after tonight I won't need him any more. Thanks to you, I now have Christ again. Thank you for showing me my need."

Following one message and demonstration the president (a Hindu) of one of the universities in India, said to the audience "the message which Mr. Kole gave tonight is one which we must think and rethink. Every student in India needs to hear this message and respond to it. In this ancient land of India we need a resurgence of our spirits and tonight I believe that the spirit of Jesus Christ is the answer to the problems of India and of the entire world." One student said, "I heard André Kole speak last night and my whole life was changed. For the first time I accepted Jesus Christ as my personal Savior. Never before had I experienced anything like this. My life has been more like dying than living. I have used and abused drugs. I was an honor student in high school. At eighteen I had to give up an illegitimate child. At nineteen I was arrested on three felony counts for sale and possession of narcotics. When I turned twenty-one last month I felt more like being buried than coming of age. Something deep inside drew me to the Campus Crusade for Christ meeting. Last night when I heard André speak I truly believed for the first time and asked Christ to come into my life. This is a decision that I have tried to make for the last three years and failed to do alone. Now I would just like to thank you and André and everyone else involved for making this possible. Believe me, your words are not wasted."

It was Bal Week (Easter vacation) and approximately 30,000 students from California and surrounding states crowded the sunny southern beaches of Balboa and Newport Beach. They were there for a ball, sun, sex and surf. For years Bal Week had been one of the biggest headaches for the local police as thousands of students became involved in all kinds of delinquencies, including sex, dope, drunken brawls, and vandalism.

Dick Day, our Orange County campus director, believed that something should be done about taking the claims of Christ to these thousands of students. As he sat in my office one January day he outlined a strategy. It called for taking several hundred of our staff and students into the Balboa area where they would live in the homes of adult friends. The morning hours would be spent in training the staff and students to understand how to live in the control and power of the Holy Spirit of God and how to communicate their faith in Christ effectively with these thousands of "beachcombers." The afternoons and evenings were to be spent in personal and group contacts with the students.

The results were startling and phenomenal. Contacts were not hard to make. There were plenty of people who had nothing to do but sit and listen. Trained students with clipboards, student surveys, and several *Collegiate Challenge* magazines, Van Dusen letters and *Four Spiritual Laws* booklets would divide and conquer as they sat down in their swim trunks and proper beach attire next to a sun-baked coed or young man. Thousands of students responded. The impact was so great that delinquency and vandalism were greatly lessened, and before the end of the week the police were giving the violators of the law the alternative of going to jail or talking with a member of the Campus Crusade for Christ team.

In a converted bar called The Hunger Hangar several members of the team were available to provide refreshments and to give personal counsel to hundreds of lonely students who were looking for someone to talk to about the things of God. Across the front of the temporary summer headquarters (the home of Dick and Charlotte Day) was hung the banner, CHRIST IS THE ANSWER. On the other side of the street a group of fraternity men in rebellion and reaction to our banner hung a sign from their apartment which read, BOOZE IS THE ANSWER. But in the course of the days that followed these men made their way one by one to the Day home, at first out of curiosity and then from a genuine interest that developed as members of the team talked to them of Christ and introduced them to the Savior. Eventually all of the young men met Christ and the BOOZE IS THE ANSWER sign came down.

Jerry was a beachcomber and a lifeguard. He had spent a lifetime building a beautiful body through physical exercise. Different members of the Crusade team spoke to him of Christ. The first time he laughed. The second time he was irritated. The third, fourth, fifth, and sixth through the tenth time (he reported later) he became increasingly angry. Then one day out of curiosity he decided to attend one of the Crusade meetings, and there the

152

Spirit of God captured him. Even though he tried to sneak away as soon as the meeting was over, in his heart of hearts he wanted to respond to Christ; fortunately, an alert team member followed him and asked him if he would not like to make his commitment to Christ. He joyfully responded because this was what he wanted to do. Later, he came to Arrowhead Springs to tell approximately a thousand other students that they should never be discouraged when those to whom they spoke the first time, or the second, or third, or fourth, or tenth time did not respond. Because, as he put it, "Had you not continued to work with me and to witness to me, I might still be wasting my life on sex, suds, sin, sun and surf. I want to thank you for telling me about Jesus Christ and insisting I give Him an honest hearing. Now that I have received Him as my Savior and Lord, He has changed my life; and I want to spend the rest of my life helping others to find Him."

A young woman knocked on the door of the Crusade house in great emotional distress. She blurted out, "I've had sex six times already this week, and I'm so sick of myself that I could vomit. I need God, and I'm told that there is someone here who can help me find Him." Soon after, she had laid her sins over on the Lord Jesus and had received Him as her Savior. Having come in tears, she went away rejoicing.

From its beginning at Balboa and Newport Beach under the enthusiastic and able leadership of Dick and Charlotte Day, the ministry soon spread to other beaches. Daytona Beach, Ft. Lauderdale, Panama City, Ocean City, Lake Tahoe, Cape Cod, Santa Cruz, Colorado River, and other resort areas became the scene of Campus Crusade for Christ activity, as thousands of staff and students invaded these areas to give witness to the living Christ.

One day, just after I had arrived at my hotel room on the beach at Daytona, a young man knocked on the door of my room and asked if he could retrieve his key. It seemed that he had tossed his key from the patio area on the ground to the third floor, but he had missed the third floor and his key had fallen on my terrace on the second floor. Knowing that God makes no mistakes and sensing that here was a lad whom God had prepared, I invited him in and he found his key. Then I asked him if he had a few moments to talk. As we chatted together I explained to him the love of God and His forgiveness made possible through faith in

153

Jesus Christ, as contained in the *Four Spiritual Laws* booklet. When I finished he told me this moving story: "I grew up in the church. My mother and father are very devout Christians. But I have rejected Christianity. For some reason I have not found satisfaction and fulfillment in the church. My parents did not want me to come to Daytona. They knew that I would be involved with the wrong crowd. But in violation of their wishes I came anyway. And now, of all the places in the world, you should be here to confront me with what my mother and father have told me all these years. Surely, God has arranged this meeting."

We knelt together and prayed, and this young modern-day prodigal who had been running from the Lord surrendered his heart to the Savior. Stories such as this could be told by the thousands, as God in His sovereignty, love, and grace reaches out through His children—men and women who are filled with His Spirit—on the beaches, in the parks, in the ghettos, wherever men are available to make His love known and to woo others to accept our Savior.

There are many different attractions that make these special Easter and summer vacation projects successful. André Kole and the New Folk have been featured with outstanding success in the various night-time programs. One way that we have found to be extremely successful in drawing large crowds is to have the hundreds of staff and students meet for special prayer and instruction an hour or so prior to the big beach rally and then to parade to the beach, inviting everybody they meet to join with them. Soon several hundred become several thousand as all spectators are invited to join in marching to the rally site.

The staff of Campus Crusade for Christ is vitally concerned with the racial, social, and political issues that are of such great concern to the students. We believe that as Christians we have definite moral and social responsibilities though our first and major thrust is in the area of evangelism. For several years Campus Crusade for Christ has been involved in seeking to help solve the tension in the inner city areas in Miami, Florida, and Newark, New Jersey. The students and staff who participate in these projects engage in personal evangelism, block parties, athletic clinics, music action teams, home Bible studies, personal spiritual training, and relevant community involvement.

The following are comments from individuals who have participated in the Campus Crusade training programs in the ghettos: "The pastor of a black church who received training with staff and students led four men to Christ this week, two in a shoeshine parlor, two in a bar. He said, 'This week I have led four men to Christ within two blocks of my church, and one week ago I would never have believed it to be possible. Praise the Lord!'" From another: "Three of the fellows who received Christ with me earlier this summer have led several others to Christ already."

Many other challenging and unusual situations have developed as a result of our inner city ministry. From Miami, Florida, came the following report: "One evening we were taking home some fellows who had been over for dinner. Two of them were Christians and were becoming more involved in the work. We had just let Tom off at his house and were driving away when we noticed in the rear-view mirror some guys who were gathering around him pushing and shoving. Naturally we backed up, thinking he was in real trouble. It turned out that they were friends of his. They thought we were a group of guys looking for trouble, but we quickly assured them that we had just come back to meet them.

"Tom jokingly suggested that we share the Four Laws with his buddies. One said he was allergic to religion as we began to pass out *Four Laws* booklets. Gary spoke to them through questions like, 'Do you believe there is a God?' 'Is He interested in you personally?' We ended up with prayer and four of the five received Christ. We asked if they wanted to get together, to which they responded with an enthusiastic yes. The next night there were fifteen. Six had been rounded up by the guy who was supposedly allergic to religion.

"We have continued to this day, having discussions in front of Tom's house three or four times a week at 10:00 P.M. We have had the privilege of seeing eight men trust Christ. What amazes us most is these guys were tough (carrying knives) and yet when Christ worked in their lives, we became the best of friends."

Six hundred primarily white staff and students at Arrowhead Springs accepted the invitation of Dr. Edward Hill, pastor of the

Mt. Zion Baptist Church, and of a number of other Negro pastors in the Watts district of Los Angeles, to spend the weekend witnessing in the homes and churches of the area. Church members in the area provided food and lodging for the staff, entertaining them in their homes and worshiping with them in their churches. On this never-to-be-forgotten weekend more that 1,000 black people made salvation decisions for Christ. The love of God flowed freely, uniting blacks and whites together in the Lord Jesus Christ.

The young man who is responsible for these beach and inner city projects is Eddie Waxer, special assistant to the president. Eddie has had a remarkable experience with Christ which he shares freely with great effectiveness. "Have you ever become lost in the deep woods and feared that you might never find your way out? That was the feeling which possessed me for most of my life. I wanted very much to lead a good life, but my human controls were never capable of achieving it. My background was Judaism. At age thirteen I had my bar mitzvah, the religious ritual in which a Jewish boy becomes a man. I did not find peace or satisfaction in rituals and rejected all religion. During spring vacation in my sophomore year at Michigan State I met a girl who was very attractive, very intelligent and a fine tennis player. One night after a tennis match we talked about Jesus Christ. She was the first person my own age I had ever met who talked about Jesus Christ as if she knew Him. I was amazed that such a sharp girl held such beliefs. She told me about Campus Crusade for Christ, and I decided to attend a College Life meeting to find out what kind of fanatics they were. I was surprised to find a group of impressive men and women representing all areas of campus life. From the very first meeting I had a desire to learn more about Christianity. For the next few weeks I met with the local director of Campus Crusade, and we discussed the Scriptures and talked about what Christ could do in my life. The issues soon became clear to me. One night I knelt in prayer and opened my heart, asking Jesus to come in. The following morning I woke up happy for a change, and some of the fellows on my floor remarked about my new attitude. I had a new enthusiasm and interest for life that I had never known before. During that term I asked the Lord to calm my mind and let me concentrate upon my studies. With His help my grades improved, my dating life took on new meaning, and my newly found enthusiasm allowed me to enjoy athletics more. No longer do I have to strive to reach my goals. Now I have someone in my life who directs it for me. Jesus Christ has promised, and I have found Him to be true. "I will not in any way fail you *nor* give you up *nor* leave you without support. [I will] not, [I will] not, [I will] not in any degree leave you helpless, *nor* forsake *nor* let [you] down, [relax My hold on you].—Assuredly not!" [2]

Then there is the birth of The New Folk, Campus Crusade for Christ's singing group.

Two hundred of our staff and students convened at Ohio State University for Operation Otherside, which was designed to saturate the campus of some 40,000 students with the claims of Christ. There I heard an outstanding singing group known as the Christian Minstrels, who had come from the University of Minnesota as a part of the Campus Crusade for Christ staff and student group under the direction of Ted Martin, then the director of the campus ministry for that area. The members asked me if I thought there might be a place for them in the ministry of Campus Crusade for Christ. As we talked and prayed together about such a possibility, I felt impressed to invite the entire group to come to Arrowhead Springs for training that summer.

Later in the summer I asked Jimmy Williams, a music major in college and an outstanding musician with a beautiful singing voice (now our southwest regional campus director), if he would be responsible for training the singing group. He agreed to do this. During the course of the summer, the name was changed to The New Folk. After their training, the members took off for their first year of traveling and visited 125 college and university campuses across the United States. God blessed their ministry in a remarkable way and literally thousands of students were introduced to the Savior.

The following year, because of the overwhelming demand for The New Folk, more personnel were added to staff two traveling New Folk groups. One was called The New Folk East and the other, The New Folk West. During the year 1967–68 more than 100,000 people heard these groups sing and give witness to their faith in Christ on approximately 250 college and university

157

campuses. In addition to their campus ministry, they were invited to join "the action" at Sun Valley, Idaho, near the ski slopes; on the Colorado River, and on the beaches of Panama City, Ft. Lauderdale, Daytona Beach, Balboa, and Newport. The New Folk soon became known as the "group that is where the action is." In 1969 they appeared on the Mike Douglas show and taped the Campus Crusade for Christ television special already mentioned. More than 270,000 people saw them on the stage and millions viewed them via television. Thousands responded to the challenge to commit their lives to Christ.

In addition to The New Folk, the Forerunners, another singing group, represent Campus Crusade for Christ in Europe where for the last two years its members have presented the claims of Christ in country after country to tens of thousands of students.

In reporting the Forerunners' warmly received performances in the Finnish cities of Helsinki, Tampere, Jyväskylä, and Turku, the papers said, "The Forerunners sing of a revolution of love in a world of hate." Wherever the Forerunners appeared, Finnish students thronged to hear the good news of Jesus Christ in word and song.

On the Forerunners' first night in Helsinki 1,000 people packed the city's foremost auditorium; on the last night in Tampere, an overflow crowd of 300 listened from outside the concert hall after all the seats had been sold. In Turku, one man said, "I have never before seen so many people turn out for any event in Turku." Averaging between 1,000 and 2,000 a day, the Finnish audiences were the most thrilling and enthusiastic of any to which the Forerunners have sung in Europe.

Even more exciting than their response during the concerts, was the eagerness of the students to question the group members concerning their faith in Jesus Christ. In Tampere, the leader of a large humanistic youth movement confessed that despite all of his attempts to find reality and meaning in working for the betterment of all men, he still found that there was a gaping emptiness within. After he received Christ into his life he wrote, "You and your music really got across to me like nothing has ever done before. It's a wonderful relief to have found the answer." A girl in Jyväskylä said in faltering English, "You make us glad you are here. Thank you for coming here to sing and tell us these things.

I know I have found the Christ. I know Jesus now, and God. I am so happy." A boy in Turku said, "If this message is true, it is the greatest news in the world, and I would want to spend my life telling others about it."

These students and many like them have expressed a desire to be part of a growing, moving body of students who want to see a spiritual revolution take place in Finland. Finnish students, like all European students, differ from their American counterparts only superficially. What has impressed the Forerunners is that wherever they have sung, from Berlin to the Winter Olympics at Grenoble to the London School of Economics, men and women, although culturally different, are spiritually the same. Without Christ, they are empty.

We have found that not only is Christ sufficient for Americans and their problems, but that there is no political structure, no social problem, no personal need anywhere for which Christ is not the answer. Indeed, as the Forerunners take their message to the cities and universities of Europe, students are coming to grips with the fact that Christ is "the way, the truth, and the life." [3] While in Finland, the Forerunners taped a TV program to be televised nationally at Easter; this in Europe, a continent where gospel music had not been well received.

Some Christian and secular leaders have called the Forerunners the most outstanding singing group in all of Europe. Whether this be true or appropriate, their music is catching the ear of European students and their message for Christ is getting through. Thousands are responding to the claims of our Lord.

It is the objective of the music ministry of Campus Crusade for Christ to present the ageless love of God and the exciting message of Jesus Christ to a generation that is largely unresponsive to the traditional approach. The program is designed, therefore, to attract high school and college students, to keep their attention with the sound they enjoy and are accustomed to, and to present Jesus Christ to them in a way that communicates to their needs and their desires.

One student at a recent concert commented, "All the top professional groups have exploded my mind with questions. This group with their exciting new beat have for the first time satisfied me with the answers." One angry SDS member sat in the back row at one of The New Folk musical concerts on his campus. He hated the Establishment and was committed to its destruction, but as he listened to The New Folk something happened inside and hate turned to love. Today this young man is a disciple of Jesus Christ, helping to carry the message of God's love and forgiveness to other students.

18

Into All the World

Dr. Joon Gon Kim, one of Korea's outstanding educators and Christian leaders, was enjoying the evening with his family. It was springtime and the rain was falling gently as the family was sharing the events of the day. Suddenly without forewarning or provocation, an angry band of Communist guerrillas invaded the village, killing everyone in their path. The family of Dr. Kim was not exempt. In their trail of blood the guerrillas left behind the dead bodies of Dr. Kim's wife and his father; he himself was beaten and left for dead. In the cool rain of the night Dr. Kim revived and fled to safety in the mountains with his young daughter. They were the sole survivors.

Dr. Kim is a man of God and he had learned from Scripture to love his enemies and pray for those who persecuted him. What was he to do? What was to be his attitude concerning those who had snatched his dear ones from his side—his beloved wife and honored father? The Spirit of God impressed upon Dr. Kim that he was to return to the village, seek out the Communist chief who led the guerrilla attack, tell him that he loved him and tell him of God's love in Christ, and seek to win him for the Savior. This he did, and God honored his obedience. Dumbfounded, the Communist chief knelt in prayer with Dr. Kim and committed his life to Christ. Within a short time a number of other Communists were converted to Christ and Dr. Kim helped to build a church for these and other Communists converts.

The name of Dr. Kim became known throughout South Korea,

161

but this humble, scholarly, servant of God was not satisfied. He wanted to help evangelize his whole nation for the Savior. Indeed his vision reached far beyond Korea to the whole of Asia, and he believed that his people, the Koreans, could help evangelize the whole of the Orient. Though he was a pastor of a large church, one of the largest in Korea, and had finished his theological studies in Korea, he came to the United States for further graduate study, working toward an advanced degree at Fuller Theological Seminary.

Upon meeting Dr. Kim at Fuller in 1958, I was challenged by his dedication to Christ, his humility and his vision, and together we covenanted with God that we would seek to help evangelize Korea. This was in keeping with the original vision that God gave me the night Campus Crusade for Christ was born. When I laid before Dr. Kim my strategy for the world, he responded by agreeing to launch the ministry of Campus Crusade for Christ in Korea and to be our first national director overseas. During the ensuing twelve years that followed, thousands of students have been introduced to Christ and have reached out to help influence hundreds of thousands more. So great has been Dr. Kim's influence that he has been the featured speaker at the last two presidential prayer breakfasts. The President of Korea frequently seeks his counsel and spiritual encouragement.

From the beginning, Campus Crusade for Christ has believed that the national can do a better job of reaching his own people than can the missionary. The national does not have the problems of language and culture that confront the missionary. However, we strongly believe in the importance of the missionary, so long as he is willing to serve the national. Dr. Kim and all overseas directors who have joined us since 1958 have been indigenous leaders. They have been trained and instructed in the philosophy, techniques and strategy of Campus Crusade for Christ, and we stand ready at all times to assist them in reaching their own people. Within a relatively short period of time, Dr. Kim was established in the ministry and was recruiting and training other nationals to join with him to help reach students of Korea for Christ. His has been the most remarkable student ministry in the history of Korea.

As literally thousands of students have been introduced to Christ since the beginning of the Campus Crusade ministry in Korea,

162

many of the students have found that Christians are already assuming leadership in the business, professional, political and religious life of Korea. Not the least spectacular of these activities is a social service program comparable to a Christian peace corps in which scores of student doctors, dentists and other similar qualified students go in teams to the rural farm and village areas where they provide medical, dental and other helpful services to the masses in the name of Jesus Christ. Evangelistic meetings are also held, and thousands of Koreans have been introduced to the Savior through this type of program.

The world to which our Lord has commissioned us to go is now populated with more than 3,500,000,000 people. We are told that if all the people of the world were to stand a yard apart in a continuous line, the line would stretch out more than one and a half million miles. We are told that this population will double in the next thirty years by 2000 A.D. It is estimated that there are some 224,000,000 Protestant, 585,000,000 Roman Catholic, and 142,000,000 Eastern Orthodox followers of Jesus Christ. There are 453,785,000 Muslims; 395,191,000 Hindus; 350,835,000 Confucianists; 161,856,000 Buddhists; 67,155,000 Shintoists; 51,305,000 Taoists; 13,121,000 Jews; and 924,139,000 who do not subscribe to any major religion. It should be explained that although most of China's 710,000,000 people are nominally Confucianists, with a number of Buddhists and Taoists, most of them should, for all practical purposes, be listed as Communists.

Nine percent of the world's population speaks English; 91 percent of the world does not speak English; 90 percent of the world's Christians come from the 9 percent who speak English; 10 percent of the world's Christians come from 91 percent who do not speak English; 94 percent of the ordained preachers of the world minister to the 9 percent who speak English; 6 percent of the ordained preachers in the world minister to the 91 percent who do not speak English; 96 percent of the church's income is spent among the 9 percent who speak English; 4 percent of the church's income is spent among the 91 percent who do not speak English. The United States represents 6 percent of the world's population. We own over 50 percent of the world's wealth. We spend many times more on alcohol and tobacco than we do on the entire religion, welfare and foreign missions cause.

163

For example, last year we spent $11,100,000,000 on alcoholic drinks, $8,100,000,000 on tobacco, $5,791,000,000 on religion and welfare, $3,500,000,000 on pets, $210,000,000 on dog food and care, and only $192,000,000 on foreign missions. It is interesting to note that in 1903 communism was born with 17 supporters. Communism now dominates almost half the world's population and the rest is infiltrated by it. American Communists spend 38 percent of their gross income for their cause; American Christians spend less than 1 percent of their income for foreign missions which is less than $3 per individual per year.

With this kind of dedication we are reaching only approximately two million additional people each year, which, when one considers the population increase of 65 million per year, means that only one out of thirty of the world's population increase is being reached for Christ. On the world's mission field there are 43,000 Protestant missionaries occupying some 130 fields. Protestant church membership in the United States is 67,000,000 and 8,000,000 in Canada. The missionary to church members ratio is 1 to 2,500. As one considers the world's need, there are approximately 3 million villages in the world without a single resident gospel witness.[1]

Considering these statistics, one is overwhelmed with the magnitude of this task, but the problems that faced the first century Christians were infinitely greater. When Jesus commanded us to go into all the world and preach the gospel and make disciples of all nations, He promised to go with us and because all authority in Heaven and earth is His, we can go to each of the 210 countries and protectorates of the world with the absolute confidence that the One in whom dwelleth all the fullness of the Godhead will go with us bodily and supply our needs. Thus the very thing He came into this world to accomplish—to seek and to save the lost and to communicate His love and forgiveness to all men—will be fulfilled.

Our present director in Mexico, Sergio Garcia, highly recommended as a young man with tremendous ability, flew in from Mexico City to participate in our staff training while we were still at Mound, Minnesota. He was the national oratorical champion, a brilliant student, and a dedicated Christian. However, it was immediately apparent that Sergio was aware of a great need in his life. By his own admission, he was certainly not ready to take

164

responsibility for leading a ministry like Campus Crusade for Christ in any situation, least of all, in the great country of Mexico.

During the first two days Sergio was exposed to our emphasis on the ministry of the Holy Spirit, which is basic to all of our teaching. You will remember that Jesus commissioned the disciples to go into all the world and to preach the gospel. But He admonished them to wait in Jerusalem until they were endued with power from on high. ". . . ye shall receive power, after that the Holy Ghost is come upon you: and ye shall be witnesses unto me both in Jerusalem, and in all Judea, and in Samaria, and unto the uttermost part of the earth." [2] Paul admonishes the church in Ephesus and all believers through the centuries, including our own generation, to be filled with the Holy Spirit.[3]

When Sergio Garcia heard this message he realized that this was what was wrong with his life. He needed the power of God, the Holy Spirit, to perform the ministry of God, the work of God. That night, claiming by faith the *command* to be filled with the power of the Spirit and the *promise* that if we ask anything according to His will, God will answer,[4] Sergio was filled with the Spirit by faith. His life was absolutely transformed. Wherever he went thereafter scores and hundreds felt the impact of the life that was aflame for God. Today Sergio, with his wife, Sylvia, is national director for Campus Crusade for Christ in Mexico, and is one of four regional directors for all of Latin America, where he is being greatly used of God.

In Mexico City one former Communist student said, "I thought that Karl Marx was the greatest revolutionary, but now I see that the greatest revolutionary is Jesus Christ." A young Panamanian guerrilla revolutionary received Christ and in spite of danger to his own life, shared this with four others in his Communist cell group. They all trusted Christ and are now growing in Him. They found that Christ is the only true answer.

Centro Chula Vista located in beautiful Cuernavaca, Mexico, the "Garden City of Latin America," is our Latin American training center for evangelism. In a year-round training program, this Latin American Formation Center trains our staff and students and laymen to be more effective in helping to evangelize the whole of Latin America for our Savior. Guillermo Luna, who with his wife, Olinda, is director of our ministry in Guatemala, is also regional director of the southern countries of South America, as well as director of the training center at Chula Vista.

Nestor Chamorro was a Communist and served as professor of biochemistry at the University of Valle in Cali, Colombia. When Nestor met Jesus Christ his life was dramatically changed. He saw the fallacy of the Marxist doctrine and began immediately to influence the lives of other Marxists. In the meantime he continued his studies at the Latin American seminary in Costa Rica, from which he graduated. He and his wife, Betty, then joined our staff to direct our Colombian ministry. Nestor also serves as one of our regional directors for Latin America. Among the many thousands whom he has introduced to Christ are hundreds of former Communists.

Four of our Latin American directors are former Communists. One of those former Marxists whom Mr. Chamorro influenced for Christ was Osman Soto. Osman and his wife, Hilda, now direct our work in Panama.

Miguel Barahona, with his wife, Grace, directs the ministry in Honduras. He is a graduate civil engineer from the National University of Honduras in Tegucigalpa. He is presently serving as administrator for the Latin American Formation Center.

Ladislao Leiva was a professor of biology at the National University in El Salvador and resigned that position to direct the ministry of Campus Crusade for Christ in that country. With his wife, Dolores, he is presently serving as regional director for Central America. He is also dean of students for the Latin American Formation Center.

Benjamin Carrillo, with his wife, Bertha, served as one of the leaders in the Bolivian national church for many years. As coordinator of the associated student groups in Bolivia, he now directs this ministry in his country.

De los Santos Jara is a graduate of the National University of Paraguay with a degree in law. Following his graduation he was a professor at the university before he and his wife, Nilda, came to direct the work in Paraguay.

Luis Perfetti has his degree in law and his wife, Elida, was a dentist. Prior to joining the Campus Crusade ministry, where he is now director of the ministry in Argentina, he served as principal of a Christian high school in Buenos Aires.

166

Manuel Simoes, with his wife, Priscilla, is director in training for the country of Brazil. Before joining the staff he was a pastor of a Presbyterian church in his country.

Roberto Azzati was a pastor in Argentina and his wife Beatriz was a dentist. Roberto has his degree in law. He and his wife are now directing the work in Uruguay.

Jim Thurston, an international director from the United States, is now seeking to recruit and train nationals to give leadership to the work in Chile. Similar works are being conducted in Ecuador and Venezuela to train staff and associate staff.

Bob Kendall, former athletic standout in Canada who was offered professional contracts in football and baseball upon graduation from high school, received Christ under the ministry of Billy Graham and continued his studies at Bob Jones University. He and his wife, Joan, have been members of the Campus Crusade for Christ staff for fifteen years and he has served as campus director of this ministry in Michigan, Oklahoma, and Texas. Since 1962 he has been director of Latin America affairs. Recently he assumed the responsibility for the Campus Crusade ministry in his native country, Canada. Under the leadership of Bob Kendall, the most strategic event in the history of our ministry in Latin America was undertaken in the fall of 1969.

At that time the directors and a number of the staff from fourteen countries of Latin America and from Spain were brought to our Latin American Formation Center in Mexico for a year of intensive training in evangelism. The purpose of the Formation Center is to impart to the national directors and national staff Bible doctrine, and practical campus training in the how to's of the Campus Crusade for Christ ministry, especially in the areas of evangelism and follow-up, Bible study, several strategic books of the Bible, family relationships, personal maturity and development, and on-campus experience with other staff in winning and discipling men. This type of training is little known and is not available anywhere in Latin America. The need for this intensive training was expressed by the national staff themselves and already many of them have stated that this training has revolutionized their lives and given them a new perspective and challenge to reach their respective countries for Christ. Key students, laymen and some staff are continuing the ministry in almost all of the

167

countries. This experience and responsibility has already challenged a number of them to consider full-time Christian work. As one student from Bolivia wrote to his director, "Each day I see the necessity of fully preparing to win students for Christ; I believe this is the vocation to which the Lord is calling me."

Not long ago, I had the opportunity to meet with twelve of our national directors at an Asian conference in Japan. For a week we met in a beautiful mountain retreat near Tokyo.

Again and again my heart was warmed and my confidence that the Great Commission would be fulfilled in our generation was increased, as I heard these anointed men speak of their faith and of their personal experiences with Christ as they have directed the ministry of Campus Crusade for Christ in their respective countries. I wish it were possible to tell in detail the remarkable qualifications of these and all of the other directors from forty-three countries around the world. Some of them are outstanding leaders of their countries, and all of them believe with me that the Great Commission can be fulfilled in our generation, none of them more enthusiastically than Geoffrey Fletcher.

Before becoming our director for Australia, he was the director of evangelism for the Anglican Diocese of Sydney. It is interesting how I met Geoff. One of the Sunday school publications carried a brief article about the Four Spiritual Laws. Geoff's wife, Diane, read the article and wrote to Arrowhead Springs for additional materials. They received a price list and samples of various items, and began to study everything that Campus Crusade for Christ had produced. With the passing of months, they became increasingly interested in the ministry of Campus Crusade for Christ, and when Geoff was selected as a delegate to the World Congress on Evangelism in Berlin, he arranged his schedule so that he could come by way of Los Angeles on his way to Berlin. While here, he shared some of the exciting things that God was doing in Australia. An invitation was extended to me and a team of laymen to hold a citywide Lay Institute for Evangelism in Sydney at the famous Saint Andrew's Cathedral, and in Melbourne at St. John's Toorak. There we had opportunity to see approximately 2,500 people from hundreds of churches who were trained to be more effective in their lives and witness for our Savior. Even more exciting, God called Geoff to direct this ministry in his country to give leadership

168

in reaching approximately fourteen million Australians with the same kind of training so that they in turn could help evangelize and disciple the whole of the Orient.

Then I would like to introduce Ananda Perera our director for Ceylon and his wife, Edna. A converted Buddhist, Ananda received his training at Calvin College and Seminary in Michigan where he earned his B.D.

Our director for Indonesia, Ais Pormes, an outstanding young businessman who was reached for Christ, received his training at Melbourne Bible Institute in Australia and later at Biola College in California, from which he received his B.A. As head chaplain to the Christian Labor Union, which played a major role in the overthrow of the Communist government and the disbanding of the Communist party in Indonesia, he is recognized as one of the leaders of that country, where God is doing such great things in our day. His wife, Tina, ministers with him.

Sam Arai who with his wife, Yoshi, directs in Japan, came to know Christ while a student majoring in chemistry at Tokyo Metropolitan University. He responded to the gospel the first time he heard it. Later, at Wheaton College he received his master of theology degree; he is recognized as one of the outstanding youth evangelists in all of Japan.

James Tai became pastor of one of the oldest Presbyterian churches in Taiwan following his seminary graduation. As director for Taiwan, he and his wife, Minnie, are making an impact for Christ throughout Taiwan and other Chinese populated areas of Asia.

Guillermo Bergade, director for the Philippines, was an outstanding, well-loved pastor for nine years. Greatly used in personal evangelism, he received his bachelor of theology degree from Silliman University in the Philippines and his master's degree in Biblical Studies from Trinity Evangelical Divinity School in Illinois. Today, thousands of Filipinos are being confronted with the claims of Christ through the ministries of Guillermo and his wife Betty, and other members of their staff.

David Hock Tey is Chinese. He and his wife Mary, are now directing the work in Malaysia and are looking forward to and praying for the day when they will be able to help lead thousands of Chinese back into mainland China with the good news of the gospel.

Adel Masri, was an outstanding pastor in Beirut, Lebanon, where God was using him in a special way to reach the students of that strategic Middle Eastern country. Now, as our directors, he and his wife, Duha give full time to that objective.

Thomas Abraham, director for the state of Kerala, India, is a graduate of the Western Conservative Baptist Theological Seminary in Portland, Oregon, where I first met him. Today he and his wife, Molly, are making a vital and powerful impact for Christ in India.

In Singapore, Kent and Diane Hutcheson, international representatives, left a fruitful ministry to the collegians of America to help our Asian nationals in various evangelistic and training programs. They now live in Singapore.

The entire Asian ministry of Campus Crusade for Christ International is under the direction of Bailey Marks, who with his wife, Elizabeth, is living in Singapore. Bailey was an outstanding young businessman in Birmingham, Alabama, when God called him to this ministry. For eighteen months he served as my personal assistant and I had opportunity to see the Spirit of God work in and through him and his wife in a wonderful way. I had no idea of his success in the business world, for he was very modest about his personal achievements, until one night his father said to me, "I wonder if you realize that you have a $50,000-a-year assistant?" I was a bit surprised but not for long, as I was made aware of Bailey's training in business administration at Vanderbilt University, his role as an officer in the U.S. Navy and then finally, years of business training as vice-president of a large and successful business. Now, all of this had been put aside as he and Elizabeth had discovered something infinitely more exciting and challenging, the opportunity to help reach the world for Christ and fulfill the Great Commission in our generation.

Gordon Klenck has been a member of the Campus Crusade for Christ staff for eighteen years. A graduate of Fuller Theological Seminary, he is now director of European affairs for the Crusade ministry. He and his wife, Marci, and their two children are living in Italy.

One of Gordon's able assistants has been Bud Hinkson. Bud

was student body president of the University of Oregon and played an important part in helping to reach thousands of students in the States for Christ before joining the European staff where he, with his wife, Beverly, is now acting director for England.

Richard and Shirley Harbour are natives of England. He is now director in training under the leadership of Bud Hinkson with a view to assuming the leadership in the near future.

Frank and Judy Kifer are also assisting Gordon Klenck in the direction of the European ministry, having launched the work in Germany where they found trained nationals to take leadership. They are now helping to recruit additional staff for Europe.

Kalevi Lehtinen, director for Finland, has had a remarkable impact in the lives of thousands of students since the first year of the ministry in that country.

Bernhard Rebsch, who with his wife, Ann, is directing the work in Germany, was trained by Frank Kifer and now gives leadership in reaching the students of that strategic country.

Jan Kits, director for The Netherlands, and his wife, Nel, and his staff have been given the remarkable opportunity of playing a major role in presenting the gospel through a nationwide television program, as well as reaching students on the campus in the traditional way.

Key men are also in training for various countries of Europe and Africa, including Joel Baldari in Italy; José Monells from Spain; Solomon Asimpi, Ghana; Victor Lawson, Liberia, and Yemi Lapido, Nigeria. Also, plans are being made to launch the ministry in Switzerland, Sweden, Austria, and France.

Larry Benton, formerly an outstanding real estate developer and for some years manager of the Arrowhead Springs Hotel when it was owned and operated for secular purposes, became a Christian through the ministry of Campus Crusade for Christ four years ago. He, with his wife Beverly, is now serving Christ as administrator of overseas ministries.

Imagine my joy and excitement when I have the privilege of visiting each year with all of these national directors in their various training and strategy sessions. The challenge is great as we pray and discuss maps of the countries of the world. We claim that the Lord of the harvest will raise up laborers by the millions, and disciple them to help saturate all the 210 countries and protectorates of the world with the good news of God's love and forgiveness in Christ. What an exciting adventure and privilege.

Some may wonder where God would have them serve in helping to change the world. It may well be that some would like to know more about how they can serve Christ in the countries already named, or how they can help to launch the ministry in the remaining countries of the world where this ministry is yet to be established.

It is our strategy to take the claims of Christ to every high-school and college campus in the United States and to every state, metropolitan area and precinct. We work together with local churches and other organizations through direct mail, radio, television, films, personal contacts and group meetings. We seek in every way possible, through all the means that are available to us through modern technology and science, to introduce tens and hundreds of millions of men and women around the world to Christ. By working in cooperation with other Christian organizations, we seek to train millions of disciples to help saturate the world with the gospel.

For the present at least, most of the readers of this book are likely to be Americans. It is a humbling thing to realize that we Americans represent only 6 percent of the world's population and yet own more than half of the world's wealth. God has given this country unlimited resources and manpower and finances. Surely to whom much is given, from him shall much be required. God has called America to help bring the blessing of His love and forgiveness to the rest of the world.

There are three major ways in which to help. *First,* pray. Those who understand and experience the privilege and power of prayer will understand when I say prayer is absolutely the most important thing that one can do. As our example, our Lord is now interceding in our behalf in His place of authority and power. *Second,* go. Christians should ask God if He wants them to serve Him in another country. *Third,* help financially. Many millions—yes, even billions—of dollars are needed for recruiting and training millions of workers, providing them with the tools—literature, films, tapes—to evangelize and disciple the nations of earth.

For $5,000 an individual can become a spiritual parent of an entire country and have a spiritual investment in every person reached for Christ in that country through this ministry. The $5,000 covers the cost of recruiting and training a director for the country. Further details are available on request.

By using a map of the world one can begin to pray specifically that God will raise up in each nation a great army of men, men of His choosing, men controlled and empowered by the Spirit of God, who will be His disciples. We are praying that the day may speedily come when millions of dedicated men and women will be available for training to help fulfill the Great Commission in our generation.

19

Arrowhead Springs: A Center for Year-Round Action

A spiritual revolution requires well-trained forces and a vital, supportive ministry. World-famous Arrowhead Springs, located in the beautiful San Bernardino mountains, was acquired by Campus Crusade for Christ to meet these needs.

Dedicated as an Institute for Evangelism, Arrowhead Springs is used to train thousands of students, laymen, and pastors to be used in winning, building, and sending men and women to help fulfill in this generation our Lord's Great Commission to take the gospel to all the world. In addition, it serves as the international headquarters. The main offices for all of the field ministries, administrative and technical services, and conferences are at Arrowhead Springs, the nerve center of Campus Crusade for Christ.

Management responsibility for Arrowhead Springs and Campus Crusade belongs to a team of qualified and successful businessmen who have dedicated their lives to Christ and to helping fulfill the Great Commission through the Campus Crusade for Christ ministry.

Typical of these is Bruce Bunner, CPA, who with his wife, Ingrid, left a profitable career in business to join the Campus Crusade staff. As controller and vice-president for administration and finance, he provides able and knowledgeable leadership in a vitally important area of the Campus Crusade for Christ ministry. Bruce explains his reason for leaving business to join the staff: "Knowing Jesus Christ personally and experiencing His love and forgiveness had redirected the objectives of my life. I believe we live in a generation that is more in need of Jesus Christ than any previous one in history. For that reason I left a management position with a national firm of certified public accountants, because I wanted to invest 100 percent of my energy, professional talent and training in serving Christ through the ministry of Campus Crusade for Christ."

Bruce is assisted by a team of outstanding young men who are also dedicated to investing all of their abilities in the cause of Christ. Ron James, with his wife, Shirley, came to us from a leading aerospace firm to head up our vital computer operations. Wally Bromberg, with his wife, Evelyn, is responsible for the Arrowhead Springs Hotel conference services. He joined Campus Crusade after serving as vice-president and treasurer of a millwork manufacturing and distributing corporation. Payson Gregory and his wife, Dorothy, have been on our staff for seven years. Payson was formerly involved in mail ordering and in a small publishing business which he helped to establish. He is now coordinating our graphics and production departments. Felix Kinne and his wife Caroline left his peppermint and spearmint farm in Washington to head up the maintenance of the Arrowhead Springs property. Two women are also in positions of responsibility under Bruce's supervision: Breta Bate, who has skillfully directed our accounting department for twelve years; and Doris Ryen, a former social worker and a staff member for seven years, directing our personnel department.

These together with many other qualified, dedicated individuals who are totally committed to Jesus Christ and are bearing fruit in His power, are the force that makes Arrowhead Springs the bustling, productive, exciting, *living* place that it is.

Arrowhead Springs is alive with impact. The 300 staff members, because of their direct involvement with thousands of programs and materials and millions of lives in a worldwide ministry, are influencing for Christ an unbelievable number of people of other lands and cultures. While "field staff" man the front lines, execute programs, and use an increasing amount of materials, they depend on the staff at Arrowhead Springs to provide the supply line—to get the action going.

Arrowhead Springs is alive with work. As the international headquarters of Campus Crusade for Christ, it is constantly planning, organizing, corresponding, creating, revising, reporting, training, teaching, publicizing, studying, rehearsing, praying, sorting, reaching. Although Arrowhead Springs is a former resort, it is now definitely a work-place for the Lord.

Arrowhead Springs is alive with progress. The staff has been challenged to "pray for big things," to believe that God will continue to bless such a comparatively young ministry with an adequate staff (10,000 by 1976), with sufficient funds, with more equipment, with more volunteers for the Great Commission Army (5 million by 1976) to join us for Christian training and with more creative ideas that will help speed up the fulfillment of the Great Commission in this generation.

Arrowhead Springs is alive with multiplication. As an international training center, it is the location for constant teaching and training of Christians, showing them how to experience the Spirit-filled life, how to share their faith, and how to teach others to experience and share the same life of victory and fruitfulness. In other words, they are trained to multiply. This training, whether it is through a Lay Institute for Evangelism, or the Institute of Biblical Studies or a high-school conference, is also available to all of the headquarters staff.

Arrowhead Springs is alive with fellowship. The Christian family enjoys the constant fellowship of laboring together for Jesus Christ, of praying together for the field staff, of witnessing together in nearby San Bernardino and the Inland Empire, of living together in homes and apartments in the area, of relaxing together at the pool and on the tennis courts, of meeting informally for fun and Bible study and discussion. A weekly staff night, Tuesday devotions, office devotions, Thursday prayer, retreats, luncheons, and spontaneous sharing times are some of the situations in which the brothers and sisters at Arrowhead Springs unite to glorify Jesus.

Arrowhead Springs is alive with testimony. It is itself a visual miracle of God. People all over Southern California, and especially those in San Bernardino, know that Christians "have taken over Arrowhead Springs" and they have a natural interest in what goes on here. Through church work, neighborhood Bible studies and action groups, through a monthly College Life type program, through weekend outreaches and through business contacts, God is making the Inland Empire very much aware of His presence, and of His obvious blessing on Campus Crusade throughout the world.

176

greater glory to God, we have invested in the finest of electronic data processing equipment. Computer operation, key punching, programming, and systems analysis are the main responsibilities of this necessary department.

The conference services department seeks to provide warm, efficient Christian hospitality to visiting staff, students, laymen, conferees, and dignitaries. This responsibility involves hotel management, guest reception, registration for all institutes and conferences, book store operation, and food services.

The grounds operations department is another area so vital to the management and upkeep of Headquarters. Since the time the Lord first gave Arrowhead Springs to us, we have shown our gratitude and willingness to care for His gifts by organizing a full-time staff in charge of maintaining the grounds and buildings, landscaping and planning the development of new facilities. Under the direction of the grounds staff, the Arrowhead grounds become increasingly beautiful each year.

The mass media ministry serves with the belief that nothing is impossible with God. Through His use of magazines, newspapers, mail campaigns, radio, films, and TV programs, and evangelistic audiovisual aids, we are convinced that this generation can hear of the love of Jesus Christ and learn how to know Him personally.

In the art and graphics department, photographers and artists serve the mass media ministry and other departments in designing, lay-out and providing of photographs for magazines, brochures, posters, books, films and promotional materials.

Multiplying the availability of God's Word and the Christian's testimony is the scope of the printing department. Such important details as camera stripping, lay-out for printing, and bindery work are handled here—all resulting in the production of high quality materials to be used by our staff and trained volunteers all over the world.

The correspondence department has the mammoth but rewarding task of corresponding with thousands of new Christians on a regular follow-up schedule, plus maintaining the entire Crusade mailing list, and counseling by mail with both Christians and non-Christians. Although we are a large organization, we never want to lose the personal interaction that is so basic to evangelism and follow-up.

The entire Campus Crusade staff, including myself, whether we are in a headquarters office or on the campus or in a community church, are daily challenged to be all that Christ wants us to be— that is, servants living in obedience to His commands under the power of the Holy Spirit.

Together we are laboring to help fulfill the Great Commission in this generation. Every ministry, every office, every publication, every policy, every activity and every project revolves around this goal. Paul refers to this unity of purpose and sole source of strength when he says, in effect,

And there are varieties of ministries and the same Lord . . . one and the same Spirit works all these things, distributing to each one individually just as He wills. For even as the body is one and yet has many members, so also is Christ. . . . God has placed the members each one of them in the body, just as He desired. . . . Now you are Christ's body, and individually members of it.[1]

At Arrowhead Springs, there is a limitless variety of ministries and opportunities for serving the same Lord.

The administration and planning department keeps the ministry running smoothly. Through services to the headquarters offices and the field ministries, through in-depth training of new personnel and through immediate and long-range planning, they seek to se that all things are done "decently and in order." [2]

With plans for 10,000 staff and 5,000,000 volunteers for t Great Commission Army by 1976, the personnel department constantly involved in recruiting, counseling, screening, intervic ing, processing applications, selecting and placing staff, filing handling selective service problems. Its primary aim is to be u of God to place His people in strategic areas of His service.

The accounting department has been entrusted with the res sibility of caring for God's money, and consequently is in ch of administering all financial policies, receiving and reco contributions, bookkeeping, budgeting, payroll, accounts recei and payable, and administering insurance.

Consequently, we have also established a data processir partment. For greater efficiency and economy of operation an

The direct mail and mail order department holds that promptness is a part of a good testimony for Jesus Christ even when the job seems impossible. For example, in one month half a million *Four Spiritual Laws* booklets alone were sent out.

Thus, this department, which handles the mailing of all materials and letters that leave Arrowhead Springs, utilizes automatic addressing, inserting and postage equipment.

The Campus Crusade staff also includes qualified legal counsel, following the Scriptural admonition to obey the governing authorities, and to "lead a quiet . . . life in all godliness and honesty." [3] The legal office gives serious time to such things as contracts, copyrights, trademarks, corporate records and federal tax regulations.

The vital responsibility of the public relations and development department is to make sure that this organization is always Scriptural and honoring to God, by giving special, helpful attention to the friends and supporters of Campus Crusade, and also by encouraging new friends to become involved in the worldwide ministry. Campus Crusade never wants to be organization-oriented, but always centered around Jesus Christ and His glory.

The offices for the field ministries—campus, lay, high school, military, and overseas—are exciting areas of service. Daily, each office receives "epistles" from the field staff. They are letters full of news of God's work, prayer requests and business. It is the responsibility of these offices to coordinate all the ministries on the field—seeking to put the most thorough evangelistic efforts into every strategic area in the world. Because of the prayer and long-range planning of the offices, the campus staff, athletic staff and lay staff, for example, have been able to combine their outreaches and saturate whole schools and cities.

Many of the leading business and professional people of our nation are lost to creative jobs upon retirement. Multitudes of these are being challenged and called to join with us in helping to change the world. One of these is a former teacher of commercial subjects and speech. During the last six years she has volunteered her time and tremendous talent to assist me personally in vast amounts of correspondence and in the editing of special projects. I have often remarked, "I do not know what I would do without her help." No doubt, there are thousands of top executives and otherwise gifted people who would respond to similar challenges if they knew their services were needed.

Arrowhead Springs *is* alive. Here is a place where any committed Christian, no matter what his special skill or talent is, can fit in, and be used of God in a fruitful and world-changing way. In fact, we are continually praying for more individuals with secretarial, clerical and administrative background and skills— qualifications that one does not normally associate with Christian service, but that are actually indispensable to a worldwide evangelistic movement.

The headquarters staff member is in a strategic spot. He is in the heart and nerve center of a movement that is being directed and blessed by God. He is a prayer warrior for missionaries of the whole world; daily he has cause to praise God for specific miracles occurring throughout the nation. He is doing the initial, necessary Christian work that results in much more fruit on the field. Every day he is helping to plant and water thousands of seeds of the Word of God, and is reaping thirty-, sixty- or one hundred-fold.

20

The Importance of
Follow-Up

Some years ago I was in a very important meeting with approximately twelve nationally and internationally known Christian leaders, men whom God was using in a very singular way. The subject of our discussion on this occasion was how to build disciples, how to follow up new converts. All of us were exercised over this problem. This was a special problem to me for some of the young men and women whom I had had the privilege of introducing to Christ did not seem to become as excited about the Lord as I felt they should. Some even drifted away. So I came to this meeting with real concern and anticipation. I felt certain that these men who had been Christian leaders for years would provide answers to the problems of follow-up that were plaguing me. We talked for some time about how to follow up new and older converts when suddenly it occurred to me to ask each of the men present who had followed him up. To our mutual amazement, not one person in that group of nationally and internationally known Christian leaders had been followed up in the traditional sense.

In my own case, I had never once responded to an invitation, raised my hand at a meeting or prayed with anyone concerning my salvation or any other commitment to Christ. In every case, I prayed alone. I received Christ after hearing Dr. Henrietta Mears share the Apostle Paul's conversion experience on the road to Damascus. I had previously investigated the claims of Christ so that I was already convinced that He was the Son of God, the Savior whom I personally needed. At the conclusion of her message, Dr. Mears challenged us to go home and get down on our knees and ask God what He wanted us to do. I did just that. Alone in the privacy of my apartment I knelt and said, "Lord, what do You want me to do with my life?" True, that prayer was vague and not very definite or specific, but God responded to the desire of my heart and Christ came that night to dwell within me and changed my whole life.

Although none of us at that meeting had ever been followed up individually, I did discover that most of us had been followed up in group situations. For example, I became very active in the college and young adult department of the First Presbyterian Church of Hollywood. There on Sunday morning, Sunday nights and Wednesday nights and on other occasions, I met with young people of college and post-college age who studied and prayed and socialized and shared Christ together as a way of life. The inspired preaching of Dr. Louis Evans, and later of Dr. Raymond Lindquist, pastors of that church, the teaching of Dr. Henrietta Mears, and the warm fellowship of the group were used of God to help me grow and mature so that increasingly my one desire was to live for Christ, to serve Him, and to introduce others to Him. In a very real sense this is the very best kind of follow-up that a new Christian can receive.

Should we conclude from my experience and from the experience of these Christian leaders that personal follow-up is not important? No, on the contrary, personal follow-up is extremely important. As a staff, we probably spend at least ten times as much time on personal and group follow-up as we do on evangelism, even though as a movement we are dedicated to aggressive evangelism. Actually, in a very real sense follow-up and evangelism cannot be separated. I prefer to use the term "follow-up evangelism" because proper follow-up involves evangelism and evangelism involves follow-up.

In a typical campus situation the staff is trained to hold meetings in fraternities, sororities, and dormitories and wherever students are willing to gather to hear the good news of the gospel. The claims of Christ are presented and the invitation is given for those who wish to know Him, to commit their lives to Him, and to indicate their decision by giving us their names and addresses. Other individuals are reached for Christ through all kinds of meet-

182

ings, large and small, in personal interviews, in telephone interviews, through distribution of literature, and the like.

Then begins the series of follow-up meetings, which include the establishment of Bible studies and action groups in the fraternity, or in the various living groups where original meetings were held. A series of twelve follow-up letters, together with appropriate enclosure materials, explains the importance of: assurance of salvation, how to walk in the Spirit, how to pray, how to witness, the importance of the church, and other subjects dealing with the various basic doctrines of the Christian life and Christian growth.

College Life meetings, attended by both Christian and non-Christian students, are held for the combined purpose of introducing some to Christ and strengthening the faith of others. Leadership training classes are held for the express purpose of building disciples, instructing students in the Biblical concepts that lead to Christian growth and maturity, such as how to walk in the Spirit, and how to communicate your faith in Christ to others. Students are encouraged to meet in small action groups where they share their faith and encourage one another in Christian growth and witness.

However, the most effective way to engage in both evangelism and follow-up is to take the new convert with us in all kinds of witnessing experiences. As the new Christian, or the Christian who is being trained, observes the other Christian sharing his faith in Christ with others he is strengthened, and after observing the first or second witnessing experience, he will want to share his own faith in Christ. The more he does, the faster he grows.

If an individual is discouraged with his Christian witness, or if he knows other Christians who are, and wants to help them, the best way that I know for him to begin moving with God is simply to confess his sins of lethargy and fruitlessness to God. He should then thank God for forgiving him and cleansing him as He promised, "If we confess our sins, he is faithful and just to forgive us our sins, and to cleanse us from all unrighteousness." [1] Then by faith he can appropriate the fullness of God's Spirit on the basis of His *command* to be filled, [2] and of His promise that if we ask anything according to God's will He will hear and answer us. [3] He can then go out in the power of the Spirit by faith, whether or not he

183

feels like witnessing, knowing that God has heard his prayers and will use him in accordance with His command and promise. As he begins to share his faith in Christ in the power of the Holy Spirit through the use of the Van Dusen letter, the Four Spiritual Laws, the Uniqueness of Jesus, or something similar, the cold heart, the heart of unbelief, the fruitless life will come alive for Christ. In this way carnal Christians become spiritual Christians and spiritual Christians are fruitful for Christ.

Occasionally one hears, "I don't want to speak to that group because I don't have time to follow-up the converts should there be any," or, "I don't want to lead that person to Christ because I don't have time to follow him up." Such expressions or such an attitude on the part of the Christian is indicative of a failure to understand the sovereignty and grace of God. Salvation is a gift of God. The Bible reminds us, "For by grace are ye saved through faith; and that not of yourselves: it is the gift of God: Not of works, lest any man should boast." [4] We are told that God proved His love for us in that while we were yet sinners Christ died for us. Since the new birth is the result of the Holy Spirit working in the life of the believer through faith, it logically follows that Christian growth is a result of faith also. "As ye have therefore received Christ Jesus the Lord; so walk ye in him." [5]

From the very first weeks of the Campus Crusade for Christ ministry, we have placed a very strong emphasis on follow-up. I remember that Dawson Trotman, founder and for many years the director of the great Navigator movement, graciously took time from his very busy schedule to come every Saturday morning for a period of weeks to meet with new converts on the UCLA campus when we first started this ministry. I shall always be indebted to Dawson—and later to Lorne Sanny—and the Navigators for their strong emphasis on follow-up. Yet I have discovered through the years that many of those with whom I spent the most time have failed to go on for God, and others who seemed to give very little indication of going on, with little encouragement from me, have become real disciples for Christ. How do we account for this? It is still a mystery to me. I know that God expects me to do everything I can personally. He expects me to pray for the converts, and no doubt prayer for the converts, as the apostle Paul demonstrated, is one of the most important things we can do; and He

184

expects me to spend time in Bible study and prayer with the converts whenever possible. Yet, thank God the Christian growth of those for whom I am used to introduce to Christ depends upon the Holy Spirit's working in their lives, not upon my feeble, fumbling efforts alone.

I remember early in my Christian ministry when I was so greatly distressed about those who were not going on for Christ, I read the parable of the sower and this passage helped me to realize the reason many do not go on. The passage is familiar.[6] When the seeds were scattered some fell beside the path and the birds came and ate them. Other seeds fell on rocky soil where there was little depth of earth. The plants sprang up quickly in that shallow soil, but the hot sun soon scorched them and they withered and died for they had so little water. Other seeds fell among the thorns but the thorns choked out the tender blades. However, the seeds that fell on good soil produced a crop that was thirty, sixty, and even a hundred times as much as had been planted. Then Jesus explained to the disciples what He meant. In the first case, He said that the hard path where some seeds fell represented the heart of the person who hears the good news about the Kingdom and does not understand it, and then Satan comes and snatches away the seeds from his heart. The shallow, rocky soil represents the heart of the man who hears the message and receives it with real joy but he doesn't have much depth to his life and the seeds do not take root very deeply. When troubles come and persecutions begin because of his conviction, his enthusiasm fades and he drops out. The ground covered with thistles represents a man who hears the message but the cares of this life and his longing for riches choke out God's Word and he becomes unfruitful. The good ground represents the heart of the man who listens to and understands the message and produces a crop many times larger than the original—thirty, sixty, or even a hundred times larger.

The understanding of this passage helped me to accept the fact that not everybody to whom I talked was going to receive Christ, and not everybody who prayed with me to receive Christ was going on to maturity in Him. I had to leave these matters to God who loved them more than I and who demonstrated that love by sending His only begotten Son to die on the cross for them and for us all. If it is through the ministry of the Holy Spirit that men are

185

born into the family of God, then it must be through the work of the Holy Spirit that they will continue to grow.

It has been helpful to me to realize these things. There are Christians who ridicule the idea that another person can be introduced to Christ in a few minutes or that one should witness for Christ even if he cannot follow up the convert. I am sure that a careful study of the Scriptures will reveal the fallacy of both arguments. Jesus, for example, spent only a brief time, possibly only a few minutes, and probably not more than an hour or two with the woman at the well. It is likely that He spent no more time with Nicodemus, and yet we have reason to believe that both the woman and Nicodemus committed themselves to Him as their Savior and Lord. Philip, the deacon, spent only a few minutes with the Ethiopian eunuch, and yet tradition tells us that it was the eunuch who carried the gospel back to Ethiopia and planted the church in that country. After Pentecost three thousand were added to the church, and later five thousand. Could these converts have been real? Did they last? If so, how were they followed up? What was man's role? And what was the role of the Holy Spirit?

After working constantly with collegians and laymen for approximately twenty-five years, I have concluded that God has already sown the seed of the gospel in the hearts of a multitude of men and women and that they are ready to receive Christ instantly upon learning the "how to." We are to make every effort to follow up each convert. Yet, we must be careful not to usurp the role of the Holy Spirit. Even if we give of ourselves fully and completely without reservation to their growth and maturity, we must be prepared for some to fall away.

But, joy of joys, what an encouragement to see many who drift away come back to the Lord Jesus some time later. For example, I talked the other day to one of the most outstanding Christian laymen in America. His uncle, a famous theologian, introduced him to Christ. He studied for four years in one of our leading theological seminaries where the word of God was instilled in his heart. He was one of the leaders of a great Christian movement for several years and then turned to secular pursuits and began to drink, and in other ways compromised his Christian testimony. This continued for some years until finally the Spirit of God reminded him of his heritage in Christ and convicted him of his sin. He confessed his

186

sin and turned to Christ and has since become an outstanding lay evangelist for our Savior. Some years ago I spoke in a leading fraternity house at Washington State and the young man who was sophomore class president at the University of Idaho in nearby Moscow came to the meeting, where he received Christ. That night we had a wonderful time of fellowship together but I did not see him again for some years. One day I was visiting one of our leading theological seminaries when a fine young man introduced himself and said, "You won't know me but I'm the young man you introduced to Christ at a fraternity meeting at Washington State." Of course, I rejoiced to see him again and to learn, as I discovered through others, that he was one of the most vital witnesses for Christ in the seminary and that he had been a great inspiration to other students. I do not know who followed him up, humanly speaking, but I do know that the Holy Spirit through whose power he was born into Christ's Kingdom had followed him up and was in control of his life. There are thousands of other illustrations such as this that could be given.

As a result of these many and varied experiences it is my strong conviction that we should sow abundantly in the power of the Holy Spirit whenever there is opportunity. We should never fail to give witness for Christ and to seek to introduce men and women to Christ, individually or in groups. We should also seek to follow them up wherever there is opportunity, through every means at our disposal individually and in groups. However, we must remember the parable of the sower and not give up if some of those whom we seek to disciple for Christ do not continue to give evidence of new life in Christ. We must trust God with our converts. Trust Him that even those who drift away will come back to Christ again. We also need to pray faithfully in the Spirit for each convert, believing God that He who had begun a good work in them will continue until they come to full maturity in Christ.

21

How It Is All Financed

One of the questions I am most frequently asked as I speak to various groups and individuals across the nation is, "Who finances the ministry of Campus Crusade for Christ and how are funds spent and accounted for?"

At the heart of the Campus Crusade for Christ financial policy is a spiritual principle. We believe that we should take the teachings of Christ seriously. For example, He tells us not to store our profits here on earth where they can erode away or be stolen. We are to store them in heaven where they will never lose their value and will be safe from thieves! If your profits are in heaven, your heart will be there, too. We cannot serve two masters—God *and* money. We will hate one and love the other.[1] Also we are reminded that it is God who will supply all our needs from His riches in glory because of what Christ Jesus has done for us.[2] This is the logic behind our financial policy.

If God so loved the world that He gave His only begotten Son, that whosoever believeth in Him should not perish, but have everlasting life, then it is God's will that none should perish but that all should come to repentance, as the Scripture tells us. If Christ really meant it when He commissioned us to go into all the world and preach the gospel, assuring us that He would be with us, that He would never leave us nor forsake us, and that He would supply all of our needs, then it is a contradiction to all that we believe and preach if we give undue emphasis to material needs. Indeed I do not know of anyone who has ever been used

188

of God in any significant way who has placed undue emphasis on material things. Let me hasten to add, however, that there is nothing wrong with money nor with houses and lands, for that which we enjoy of material success is by the grace of God and is a gift from Him. It is how we use them, for the brief period of time in which we are custodians of them in this world, that determines their value.

Our Campus Crusade for Christ salary scale is modest, and all of us draw the same basic salary. The same financial policy applies to each staff member, including me. For example: in the beginning years of the ministry each staff member received $100 per month for nine months, with no salary during the three-month summer vacation. Later that amount was increased to $150, $200, and now unmarried staff begin with a base salary of $285 per month. That amount is increased ten dollars per month for a period of five years until a maximum of $335 per month is reached. The married staff begin with a base salary of $425, which is increased $20 per month for a period of five years until the salary is $525 per month. An allowance of $30 per month is made for as many as four children, and it is increased to $40, $60, $70, and $100 per month through the grades, high school, and college years. Each staff member is responsible for raising his own support.

In the beginning years of the ministry, until we had approximately fifty staff members, I was responsible for raising most of the support for the staff and for the entire ministry. Eventually, it became apparent that as the staff grew I would be forced to give all of my time to raising funds. I did not believe that this was what God had called me to do. As I prayed about the matter, the Lord reminded me that many hands make for light work; thus, it was decided that each staff member should be given the challenge and opportunity to raise his own support. By having each staff member enlist the help of his own church and of friends who were interested in his ministry and thus in helping to evangelize the world for Christ, we would be able to accelerate and expand the ministry much more rapidly. God blessed this new policy and although our present staff now numbers almost 1,700 (with an anticipated increase of 1,000 in the next twelve months), I am able to give my time largely to spiritual matters and to organizational concerns rather than to the raising of money.

In amazing, even miraculous ways God has met the material needs of this ministry day by day for almost nineteen years. In the beginning days when we needed a few hundred dollars, God met those needs. When our needs increased to thousands, those needs were met, and now with a need for millions, He continues to provide. We never have any extra. It is as though God is giving us our daily manna, and that is all that we need and want. If we had millions of dollars in reserve there would be a temptation to trust in material possessions, securities, bank accounts, rather than in the living God. The privilege of trusting God day after day and seeing His miraculous answers to prayer, results in a more vital, living, personal relationship and dependence upon Him.

All honorariums for speaking go to the ministry of Campus Crusade or are applied to the personal support of the individual involved. These do not constitute increases in salary, but are credited to his account, where they are available for regular salary or other needs. No staff member is permitted to solicit personal gifts of any kind (other than staff support) from anyone, though it is not against policy for staff to accept gifts of clothing, furniture, food and other items given as expressions of love, provided they are not solicited. The maximum for personal cash gifts is $50 per year per adult, or $25 per year per child, from anyone other than the immediate family. These policies are established in order to insure equitable and fair benefits for each staff member. They also encourage greater dependence upon the Lord.

Much of our support comes from churches that include staff members and the general ministry of Campus Crusade for Christ in their missionary budgets. Other support is provided by individuals, friends, and interested parties who want to have a part with us in helping to evangelize and disciple the world for Christ.

If this financial policy seems hard and unattractive, you will be all the more interested to know that God has called many men to this ministry from positions in the business and professional world in which their salaries were many times the amount of their remuneration with Campus Crusade for Christ.

You can well imagine that we have had a number of very interesting experiences and questions regarding our financial policies. Many people inquire of me, and more often of the staff, "How much does Bill Bright make?" As I have already mentioned, I draw the same salary as other staff members. In fact, because I have only two children and some staff have four or more, and because support is allowable for a maximum of four children, a number of staff draw considerably more each month than I do. Some also inquire, "Does Arrowhead Springs belong to him or to Campus Crusade for Christ?" We do not own any property. We live in a cottage on the Arrowhead Springs campus for which we pay monthly rent to Campus Crusade. Though my wife, sons, and I live from day to day, we have everything we need. Long ago I concluded that I could eat only one meal at a time and wear only one suit at a time and could take nothing with me when I died. Also, it is often tragically true that money left to loved ones can do more harm than good. Even Christians may be resentful over their share of the inheritance!

Some years ago a good friend and an outstanding Christian leader in the Houston area suggested to me that he would like to get some of his friends together and tell them about Campus Crusade for Christ with the thought that they, too, might join with him in making generous investments in this ministry. He said, "I want you to know that I am very much impressed with what you are doing, but I don't really know much about the way you operate—your organizational procedures, your finances. Before I invite my friends to get involved, I would like to send my accountant out to Los Angeles to look over your books and study your program. If it measures up, as I am confident it will, I would then feel free to invite my friends to join with me in investing in your program."

Of course we were more than happy to have him send his accountant to make this investigation. After three days of carefully and thoroughly studying our financial program, the accountant reported that there was only one thing wrong: we were living on a subsistence wage. Our friend was more than happy with what he had found. His accountant's report encouraged him to call together a group of outstanding citizens in Houston, who followed his example in making generous contributions to the ministry.

Recently, a new friend expressed the desire to make a generous contribution, but, as a good steward of the Lord's money, he wanted to know more about our organizational structure and the way we handled our finances. He, too, asked if he could send a representative to look over our articles of incorporation, our by-laws, and our financial records. If everything met his approval he would help us. A few days later his attorney arrived and spent several days making a very thorough check of our financial situation. His favorable report resulted in a generous contribution.

The board of directors is composed of able men and women who are dedicated to Christ and to the fulfilment of His command to go into all the world and preach the gospel and make disciples of all men. Board members are:

William R. Bright, founder and president

Vonette Bright

S. Elliot Belcher, Jr., chairman of board of directors and executive committee of Southern United Life Insurance Company

Bruce Bunner, vice-president, controller and treasurer

Arthur DeMoss, founder and president, National Liberty Corporation

Walter Gastil, president, Walter Gastil & Associates

Edward L. Johnson, chairman and president, Financial Federation, Inc.

Arlis Priest, president, Priest Realty and Investments

Lawson Ridgeway, president, Centennial Construction Company

Board members are responsible for policy-making decisions and, as trustees, are accountable for the finances with which the Lord has entrusted us. Each contribution is receipted, acknowledged, and prayerfully used for the purpose designated. Campus Crusade for Christ is recognized by the Internal Revenue Service as a religious, charitable, and educational organization; therefore, all contributions are tax deductible.

Special helpful instructions on how to purchase clothing, how to budget, and how to prepare tasty but inexpensive meals enable Crusade staff members to live on a level comparable to the average person who makes considerably more than, if not several times as much as, we make.

You can have a part in this worldwide strategy by investing through the missionary budget of your church; through individual contributions to the ministries of various members of the staff;

192

to our overseas ministry, our mass media ministry (publications, radio, TV, audiovisual, or other ministries, areas, or campuses.

Financial provision can also be made through properties, stocks, wills and annuities. A recent survey indicated that most adults do not have wills. God has given us a remarkable staff of qualified estate planners to assist those who desire our counsel and help regarding this type of support. And may I say, lest I be misunderstood and my motives questioned in raising the issue of financial investment, that no matter how much money is given, my salary, which I, like other staff members, must raise personally, will not be affected. The only reason I mention money is that large amounts of money are needed to help fulfill the Great Commission of our Lord. God expects those whom He has blessed with material resources to make wise investments for His Kingdom and He will hold them accountable for the way they spend His money. As the poet phrased it,

> Only one life
> 'Twill soon be past.
> Only what's done
> For Christ will last.

Information in regard to helping Campus Crusade financially may be obtained by writing to

> Campus Crusade for Christ
> Arrowhead Springs
> San Bernardino, California   92404

Personal contributions, life estates, wills, and other financial investments can help to change the world.

22

Come Help Change the World

We are living in a world of revolution. Historians speak of the present revolution as the first truly worldwide revolution in all of recorded history. In the last few years more than half of the human race has acquired new political status. Old political, social, economical and religious patterns are breaking down. Revolutionary ideas are stirring the hearts and minds of men.

This hour of unprecedented worldwide crisis demands revolutionists for Christ, men with a revolutionary vision and a strategy that works. This is the hour for which we Christians have prayed. This is the kind of crisis for which we were born. Now is the time for action. We dare not continue to follow the traditional pattern, nor to be satisfied with the mediocrity of the past. We must rethink our entire Christian strategy. We must return to the divine strategy of Scripture and of first century Christianity.

Because of the urgency of the hour, Campus Crusade for Christ is intensifying its program to recruit and train thousands of additional qualified staff. Tens of thousands of the most outstanding Christian leaders of our times are urgently needed to help take the message of our living Lord to students, laymen, and military personnel of every country of the world.

The Apostle Paul and the early disciples were strategists. We would do well to emulate their examples. A careful study of the strategy of Paul reveals that he was led of the Holy Spirit to proclaim the gospel of the Lord Jesus Christ in the leading centers of influence in trade, travel and learning. His converts, and those of

194

the other disciples, went from these centers into the highways and byways to proclaim the same gospel, to the extent that it was said of them that they had turned the world upside down.

The staff of Campus Crusade and the thousands of students and laymen with whom we work believe that the Great Commission can be fulfilled in our generation and have set a target date of 1980. We are mobilizing our entire movement to this end. Last year more than 500 joined the staff, and this year we are praying and trusting God for 1,000 additional new staff workers. Of course, we are sharing our need with others, too. We must accelerate our program of recruiting and training laborers to go to that portion of the 3,500,000,000 people of the world who have not yet heard of Jesus Christ. In view of the total ministry of the Body of Christ, we are also interested in recruiting staff for other Christian organizations, such as Wycliffe Bible Translators, Gospel Recordings, and other groups that are committed to translating the Bible into the languages of the approximately 1,500 tribes which have never heard the good news of God's love and forgiveness through Christ.

The source of manpower to help fulfill the Great Commission lies in the students and laymen of the world, many of whom have not yet even heard the gospel themselves. Millions of these must be reached and discipled to help saturate and disciple the rest of the world for Christ. Thousands of tomorrow's Christian leaders are not yet Christians; they are still waiting to be won for our Savior.

Jesus said that if anyone wanted to be His follower, he must put aside his own desires and conveniences and carry his cross, and follow Him closely. Whoever loses his life for Christ's sake will save it, but whoever insists on keeping his life will lose it; and what profit is there in gaining the whole world when it means forfeiting one's self? He also said He will be ashamed of anyone who is ashamed of Him and His message in these days of unbelief and sin! [1]

Men and women in great numbers are responding to that challenge in our generation. Indeed, millions of people around the world have committed themselves to be His disciples. It is the objective of Campus Crusade for Christ International to *help* establish a vital witness for our Lord on every college, university and high-school campus in each of the 210 countries and protectorates of the world, and among laymen in every walk of life. It is our goal to expose all men everywhere to the gospel, and to win, build, and send them throughout the world, through the power of the Holy Spirit, in obedience to the Great Commission of our Lord.

Campus Crusade for Christ International is concerned not only for the individual of today, but for the world that will be created by these individuals tomorrow. Today's college students, laymen, and military personnel are seeking to shape a better world. The world can be changed only as men's lives are changed. Jesus Christ is the one Person who can change a man from within, who can give meaning, purpose, and direction to men's lives.

It is not misleading to suggest that our twentieth century world can be changed in the same sense that the first century world was turned upside down. When individuals are changed in sufficient numbers, homes and communities will be changed. Cities, states and nations of the world will feel the impact of the transformed lives of the men and women who have been introduced to Jesus Christ.

When John Wesley and his colleagues were raised up of God to preach the good news of Christ in England, they were confronted with a skeptical clergy and an immoral and spiritually decadent people. Yet within the lifetime of Wesley and many of his co-workers the whole of England was so transformed that many historians recorded the dramatic changes. One historian said that in the lifetime of Wesley, England was transformed into a great sanctuary of God. Out of the great spiritual awakening in which hundreds of thousands of lives were transformed by the living Christ, England experienced a new spiritual birth. I believe that our nation will experience in our day the same transforming grace of God that England experienced in Wesley's time.

It is our objective to recruit and train 5,000,000 volunteers who will comprise the Great Commission Army. To be a member of this army, one must be committed to Jesus Christ as an act of the will. Also, in obedience to His command, one must devote his time, talent, and treasure—from the moment he awakens in the morning, until the time he goes to bed at night—as a way of life— to the fulfillment of the Great Commission. A member of the Great Commission Army is not committed to Campus Crusade for Christ, but rather to Christ and His church in a fellowship of Christian believers. To join the Great Commission Army involves no personal commitment to Campus Crusade as a movement. However, it is the desire of this ministry to make available to this army the training that has already been used of God to revolutionize the lives of thousands of people around the world.

The training we offer involves ten basic, scriptural "transferable concepts," which those who learn them teach to others in a continuous process of multiplication. Paul advised Timothy, his beloved son in the faith, to be strong with the strength Christ Jesus gave him because he would have to teach others the things he had heard Paul speak about. Timothy was further advised to teach the great truths to trustworthy men who would in turn pass them on to others.[2]

These "Transferable Concepts" are revolutionary, and they are working in the lives of multitudes. We believe they represent the kind of life-transforming qualities that must be incorporated into the life of every believer who wishes to be a follower, a disciple, of Jesus Christ.

These basic truths were learned, developed, and polished on the front line of spiritual combat on the high school and college campuses, and among laymen, clergy and military personnel of the world. I am convinced that 5,000,000 trained disciples, who are experiencing the reality of Christ's control of their lives and who know how to communicate these basic concepts intelligently to others in the power and control of the Holy Spirit, can literally change this world. These 5,000,000 will soon be 50,000,000, and eventually hundreds of millions will be introduced to Christ through these disciples, and through others whom they will disciple, by the grace and power of God.

Many of these 5,000,000 people scattered around the world will be men and women who have been trained according to this strategy in the various 176,000 precincts of America. They will be working with the local churches in programs that have been designed for and are working toward communicating the gospel to every person in every precinct, believing that the Spirit of God will win millions to Himself. Jesus said that no one could come to Him unless drawn to Him by the Father.[3]

Our experience in working with college students and laymen for almost a quarter of a century convinces us that there are tens of

197

millions of Americans and hundreds of other millions of the world's population who are waiting to become Christians. They are already spiritually ripe for the harvest. They do not need to be convinced, nor to be educated into the Kingdom. They need only to know how to become a Christian, and they will respond.

Those Christians who do not believe that men are waiting to receive Christ, however, will continue in their impotence and fruitlessness. It was said of our Savior that He could do no "mighty things" in Nazareth because of the unbelief of the inhabitants. So in our day, the spirit of Nazareth has blinded the eyes of multitudes of Christians who do not believe that God wants to, or can, work in our generation. They are content to sit on the sidelines, wringing their hands in anguish, and to say, "Why doesn't someone do something?" or "Lord Jesus, come quickly." Our Lord has commissioned us to fulfill His command. He has not promised us a bed of roses. We have not yet completed the job.

Jesus is not willing that any should perish and is allowing time for multitudes to turn to Him. Peter tells us that He is delaying His return to give us time to get His message of salvation to others. Paul says that everywhere we go we are to talk about Christ to all who will listen, warning them and teaching them as well as we know how, each one to be presented perfectly to God because of what Christ has done for each of them. This was Paul's work, and he was able to do it because Christ's mighty energy was at work within him.

The acts of the apostles are our pattern for twentieth century action. They and other Christians like them in the first century, who dedicated their lives to the Lord Jesus Christ and the fulfillment of His commission, are our examples. Can we do anything less than emulate them? Jesus Christ has not changed. He is the same yesterday, today, and forever. His great revolutionary power is as available to Christians today as it was in the first century. He is waiting for us. We are the variables. We are the ones who have short-circuited His love, forgiveness, and power to our generation.

What an adventure it is to be identified with Christ, cooperating with Him in helping to change the world that is so desperately in need of, and so ready for changing.

If you would like to have a part in helping to change the world and fulfilling the Great Commission, I invite you to join with me in this prayer:

O Lord, my God, I bow to acknowledge Your Lordship over my life. I come to give You back what is rightfully Your own. I acknowledge that I am not my own any more since I have received Christ. I belong to You. I have been bought with a price—Christ's death on the cross for me. Now, I give You my time, my talents, my treasures—all that I am and possess—that I may, like the disciples of old, be used by Your Spirit to help change the world and fulfill the Great Commission in this generation. Show me what You want me to do with my life. I pray this as an expression of my love and gratitude for all that You have done for me, and because I desire to obey You and Your command. I offer this prayer in the authority of Your only begotten Son, my Savior, the Lord Jesus Christ.

If you offered this prayer sincerely, God has already heard you and promises to direct your steps. May I encourage you to give special time to fellowship with the Lord in prayer, Bible study and witnessing, and to become active in a local church fellowship if you are not already involved. If I or the staff of Campus Crusade for Christ can be of any help to you, please grant us this privilege. We shall also be happy to send you additional materials for study, designed to assist you in your spiritual growth.

If you feel that God would have you serve Him through the ministry of Campus Crusade for Christ, opportunities to do so are many and varied. Areas of need include:

Campus Ministry, which seeks to saturate with the claims of Christ and to disciple persons in the entire academic community in the United States and throughout the world.

High School Ministry, which endeavors to evangelize the high-school students of America and to help promote the evangelization of high-school students throughout the world.

Lay Ministry, which trains laymen and women around the world how to live abundant and purposeful lives and to communicate their faith in Christ effectively to others.

Military Ministry, which seeks to win military personnel to Christ, build them in their faith, and send them to reach other servicemen for Him.

Overseas Ministry, which presents the claims of Christ and seeks to disciple students and laymen in every country of the world.

Mass Media Ministry, which confronts millions with the claims of Christ through radio, television, films, audiovisuals, and various publications in different languages.

Headquarters Ministry, which serves a vital supportive function for the entire Campus Crusade for Christ outreach. Its needs include secretaries, administrators and persons with skills or training for work in personnel, accounting, electronic data processing, conference services, housekeeping, grounds maintenance, art, graphics, photography, printing, and mailing.

As you study the above described needs, you may want to learn God's will for your life through the application of what I call the "Sound Mind Principle" of Scripture.

As a basic consideration for discerning God's will, ask yourself these questions:

(1) *Why did Jesus come?* The answer is that He came to seek and to save the lost.

(2) *What is the greatest experience of my life?* If you are a Christian, knowing Christ personally as your Savior and Lord is obviously your greatest experience.

(3) *What is the greatest thing that I can do to help others?* Your answer again is obvious: to introduce them to Christ. In doing so you enable them to experience God's love, forgiveness of sin, purpose for life, and power to live victoriously. Can you think of a greater contribution which you can make to the welfare of others?

As you attempt to evaluate the talents that God has given to you, in relation to your training, personality, and other qualities, I suggest that you make a list of the most logical ways through which your life can be used to accomplish the most for the glory of God. With the desire to put His will above all else, list the pros and cons of each possibility. The one under which you have listed the most pros will obviously direct you toward the type of service in which, through your yielded life, you can accomplish the most in continuing Christ's great ministry of seeking and saving the lost.

However, a word of caution is in order. The "Sound Mind Principle" is not valid unless certain factors exist. 1. *There must be no unconfessed sin in your life.* 2. *Your life must be fully dedicated to Christ and controlled by the Holy Spirit.* You are filled and controlled by the Holy Spirit through faith, just as you received your salvation by faith. 3. *You must walk in the Spirit or abide in Christ moment by moment.* Just as turning the steering wheel does not alter the direction of a car unless it is moving, neither can God direct our lives unless we are moving for Him.

Every Christian should take spiritual inventory regularly by asking himself this question: Are my *time,* my *talents,* and my *treasures* being invested in such a way that the largest possible number of people are being introduced to Christ? *To reach our generation for Christ, every investment of time, talent and treasure should be determined by the "Sound Mind Principle."*

At the beginning of each day, acknowledge the fact that you belong to Christ. Thank Him that He lives within you. Invite Him to use your mind to think His thoughts, your heart to express His love, and Your lips to speak His truth. Ask Christ to be at home in your life and to draw others to Himself through you. Expect God to use you more than ever before to help fulfill the Great Commission.

Can you think of any greater Leader or any greater cause to which you could dedicate the abilities God has given you? He has a plan for your life and a place where He wants to use you. Discover that place by applying the "Sound Mind Principle." We invite you, and challenge you, to join with us in helping to change the world for Christ, and in seeking to help fulfill the Great Commission in obedience to His command.

Your prayers can help to make the difference. Remember that the Scripture reminds us that if we ask anything according to God's will, He hears us, and if He hears us, He answers us. Is it God's will that the Great Commission be fulfilled? Of course. It is His command! Are His resources available to us? Yes, He has promised that they are. Then, what hinders the fulfillment of the Great Commission in our generation? One major factor: unbelief.

Our Lord could do no mighty works in Nazareth because of their unbelief.[4] So it is today. The spirit of Nazareth—the spirit of unbelief—more than any one thing is hindering a mighty movement of God's Spirit through the world and the fulfillment of the Great Commission in this generation. Remember this: "According to your faith be it unto you." "Whatsoever you shall ask in prayer believing you shall receive." "If we ask anything according to God's will He hears and answers us." On the basis of the attributes of God—His love for man, His wisdom, power, grace and faithfulness to fulfill His promises—I invite you to trust God with us for a mighty movement of His Spirit upon all the nations of the world.[5] Pray with us that a great tidal wave of spiritual blessing may engulf our world. Remember, too, you can have a part in changing the world and helping to fulfill the Great Commission through your prayers, your finances, and through the investments of your life personally.

According to your faith, be it unto you. Believe in God with us for a mighty movement of His Spirit upon the nations of the earth. Pray that a great tidal wave of spiritual blessing may engulf our world.

One final thought to take with you. The life of a true disciple of Christ is not an easy one, though it is a life filled with adventure and thrills, which one cannot possibly experience in any other way. Actually, I have thought of life like this: whether Christian or not, we are going to have problems in this life; Christian or not, we will die one day. If I am going to be a Christian at all, I want all that God has for me and I want to be all that He wants me to be. If I am to suffer at all and one day die, why not suffer and die for the highest and best—for the Lord Jesus Christ and His most worthy cause! I invite you to join with us:

COME HELP CHANGE THE WORLD.

CAMPUS CRUSADE FOR CHRIST INTERNATIONAL
(Organization Chart)

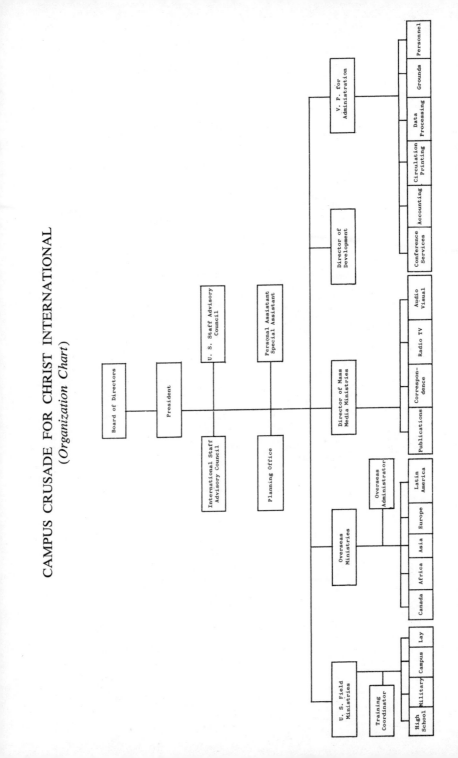

References

Chapter 3

[1] Matthew 6:33.
[2] Philippians 2:13.
[3] Acts 9:3.

Chapter 6

[1] Isaiah 57:13.

Chapter 7

[1] Romans 8:28.
[2] Hebrews 11:6.
[3] Galatians 3:11.
[4] I Thessalonians 5:18.
[5] Matthew 18:19.
[6] I John 5:14.
[7] Matthew 6:20.

Chapter 8

[1] II Timothy 2:2, *Living Letters.*
[2] Matthew 28:19, 20, *New American Standard Version.*

Chapter 9

[1] Zechariah 4:6.

Chapter 10

[1] John 6:44.

Chapter 13

[1] Luke 5:1–11, *Living Letters.*
[2] Acts 1:8.

Chapter 15

[1] John 11:25.

Chapter 17

[1] I Corinthians 9:22.
[2] Hebrews 13:5, *Amplified New Testament.*
[3] John 14:6.

Chapter 18

[1] "Facts and Figures of World Need," Bulletin of Interdenominational Foreign Missions Association.
[2] Acts 1:8.
[3] Ephesians 5:18.
[4] I John 5:14–15.

Chapter 19

[1] I Corinthians 12:4, 11–12, 18, 27.
[2] I Corinthians 14:40.
[3] I Timothy 2:2.

Chapter 20

[1] I John 1:9.
[2] Acts 1:8; Ephesians 5:18.
[3] I John 5:14, 15.
[4] Ephesians 2:8, 9.
[5] Colossians 2:6.
[6] Matthew 13:3–23.

Chapter 21

[1] Matthew 6:19–21.
[2] Philippians 4:19.

Chapter 22

[1] Luke 9:23–26.
[2] II Timothy 2:1, 2.
[3] John 6:44.
[4] Matthew 13:58.
[5] II Timothy 1:7.